I Am The Song

Your light uplifts
the world!
Blessings to you,
love Lu

I Am The Song

Recognizing the voice
of the Universe,
the magic in daily life

Lora McHenry

ISBN 978-0-9993714-4-2

Library of Congress Control Number: 2019937760

7 Stones Publishing
Gold Canyon, Arizona, USA 85118

Printed in United States of America.

This book is dedicated in love and gratitude to

Dana Strandjord, Master Teacher of energy healing, mindfulness and clarity

Mary Lee McRoberts, Master Alchemical Healer, Dancing Warrior for the Light, she guides the passage through Fourth Dimension expansion toward Fifth Dimension consciousness

Rebecca Devi, Master Teacher of perception and connecting Dimensions

Travis Taylor, Master Illuminator Bodhisattva, placing in my hand the keys to my kingdom, he holds open the door from Third Dimension experience into Fourth Dimension expansion toward Fifth Dimension consciousness

Two Notes

The Universe has asked me to tell you that you could read this book from beginning through middle to end, if that feels good to you. Or you can just flip the book open to any random page, and They want you to know that the story on that page is Their message to you on that day. Sweet!

Know that this book came to you to be part of the greater you that you are creating.

♪

The Dream, The Song

   Ohboy ohboy ohboy! A childhood dream was
coming true in far north Alaska. The only signs of
any human presence were the gravel road and the
lone long-haul truck that passed by once an hour or
so.
   I stood, elated, at the Arctic Circle. Our little
group of nine were taking each other's picture beside
the official sign way off to the side of the road.
   I felt a strong urge to be alone with the Earth
and the Air in this wild and windy place, so I stepped
across the line in the mind where the 66° 33' latitude
would be and entered the Arctic, grinning and giddy
with delight. "I'm in the Arctic! I'm in the Arctic!" I
whispered to the clouds.

   In the mild wind and the wild silence as I walked
slowly, quietly toward the top of the world, I heard a

very small sound. In a short, thin taiga fir tree a Raven moved slightly, revealing his presence to me.

"Raven, hi!" I called up to him, not actually expecting a reply. "I'm here! I'm finally here!"

"And what did you come here to find?" asked Raven.

"The edge of the Earth. The lichens and moss of the tundra under my shoes that keep sinking just a little bit toward the permafrost. My feet are not as small as the Caribou nor as sure as the Musk Ox. I came to find the winds that keep pushing the heavy clouds of whites and greys and almost-yellow. I love this sharp-edged wildness!"

"And *who* did you come here to find, Traveler?" asked Raven.

I let my mind gaze at that question for a few moments. "Me? Yes, me. My happiness in fulfilling a lifelong dream. My wonder at how wonderful the reality of the dream is. I think I came here to feel my love of me."

"Then who is the dream?" Raven asked.

"I am? I am my dream?"

"Yes, Traveler. You are everything you have

ever dreamed of being. You dreamed it all, and so it is all you."

"Oh Raven, I have dreamed for myself to be so much. Do you mean I can truly be that large?"

"Traveler, you are larger than all the thoughts together that have ever been thought. You are larger than the space beyond the sky. You are larger than light. You are as large as the Universe.

"Know that you are the music that is Consciousness. You are the endlessly unfolding Song that is Creation."

"Raven, how can I know that for sure, every day?"

"Choose to do and be what makes you love being alive.

"Pay attention to what you believe and what you feel, especially about yourself, in order to choose only what makes you feel glad to be you.

"Then trust, Traveler. Trust your intuition, which is the guidance of your heart, of the Universe, of your Angels and Spirit Guides. They have your back, and always guide you toward your highest and best good.

"When you feel as though your heart is singing, when you are in a state of joy, that is you living your highest and best good, your true purpose in life. That is your Song.

"Choose what you love. Trust your heart. That is where your truth lives."

"Lovely Raven, I am so grateful for your wisdom. Am I alone in this pursuit?"

"Never. Look for the Song in everything, everywhere, every day. It will sing to you."

"Oh Raven, thank you for being in this tree today! What a wonderful coincidence!"

"There are no coincidences and no accidents, Traveler.
I came to you today to remind you that you are your dream, and you are the Song of Creation. You are loved. You are never alone. All is well. You are the hero of your life. Pay attention, and trust."

He hopped to the top of his tree. "Hey," he called, "come do somersaults in the air with me."

"Who, me?" I asked.

"Oh that's right, you can't -- you're wearing shoes!"

Raven rose soundlessly, rising and tumbling, tumbling and rising, disappearing into the sky.

To the cool wind whispering in my ears and kissing my face, I smiled, knowing now a clearer way of seeing, a happier way of believing. "Thank you, Raven," I smiled to the sky, as I turned to walk back to my life.

~0~

Contents

The Dream, The Song

Hearing The Song

Chipmunk and Squirrel Accessories
Department
A Violet Breeze
Wild Birds
Peace
How To Compromise, In One Easy Lesson
Medicine Cat
If Wishes Were Fishes We'd Have Sushi For
Lunch
Between The Sunbeams
Communion

Learning The Song

Empathy
Dance In The Sky
Cosmic Complaint Department
Thunder Blessing
Discernment
Calling In The Ancestors
A River Rumbles, A River Roars
One More Mindful Step
Raun, Intimate Stranger
A Hero's Journey
Abundance Comes In All Kinds Of Flavors - 2
How To Forgive, In One Easy Lesson
The Social Life Of Clouds
The Mirror Me - 1
Mythticism
Dancing And The Ladybugs
All Rise!
Bliss By Dogsled
Tree At The Window
The Law Of Attraction
Comes An Ocean

If I Love You
I Am All Around You
A Flood Of Stars
I Will Help You
Breathe
Changing The Past
Say Thank You To The Nice Lady
Dreamtime In The Hills
My Porpoise
Ripples

Singing The Song

High 5!
Who's Minding The Moon?
Partners In Secret
The Flying Cat
This Time
The I Am Presence
Spiritual Dishwashing

The Faerie Who Lives On My Shoulder
Bus Stop Tree
Synchronicity Salmon
Gasping For Air
You're A Silly, Silly Mountain
Awakening
37th Avenue Robin
The Mirror Me - 2
Serendipity
Imperfect, While Perfect
Halos Of Sound
The Raphael Frequency
Changing The Future
Sugar Maple Tree
Guardian Spirit
Promises To Keep
Story Stone
To Fly
Firelight
The Apu Speaks
How To Trust, In One Easy Lesson
Apparition

I'm In Good Hands
Believe In The Little White Boat
In The Field Beyond Forgiveness
Sacred Phoenix
Light Laughing

Being The Song
I Am The Song

A Game To Play

~o~

Hearing The Song

I will repay you
for the years the locusts have eaten.
- Joel 2:25

Chipmunk and Squirrel
Accessories Department

"May I help you, sir?"

"Hi. I'd like to see a selection of tails. Maybe something in a blue plaid. Extra bushy."

"Right over here."

~o~

A Violet Breeze

One cold February day, I stepped out of the elevator in my apartment building and turned toward the hallway leading to my apartment.

From that hallway a very little boy suddenly appeared alone, walking all bundled in winter clothing, a tiny being I had never seen before.

Our eyes met. He looked serious as he walked to me, raising his arms toward my face. I smiled to him and bent down very low so my face would be level with his.

His eyes were intent as he placed his little hands slowly and very gently on my cheeks, and softly patted my face.

I felt such sweetness from him, and I began to laugh softly in sheer joy. The little boy began laughing too, as he kept pat-pat-patting my face. We were feeling so much fun and happiness together.

A woman walked into the area and gasped.

"He's so shy!" she said. "He never goes near strangers and hides behind me." I heard the surprise in her voice and I heard her words, while the little boy kept gently patting my cheeks and we two shared delight and love and laughter together.

The woman pressed the button for the elevator and quietly called to the boy. He turned from me and walked to her, putting his hand in hers.

They entered the elevator and disappeared from my life as simply as though they walked back into a fold in the Universe.

What was that?

Was that a shy little child who thought about things and decided to try out fearlessness and love?

Was that the violet breeze of God brushing my face through the little boy's hands? Was that the violet breeze of Source whispering to me, "You are loved. You are never alone. All is well. Trust."

Hmmm...

Two months and two weeks later the dream and the destiny of all my lifetimes manifested.

~o~

Wild Birds

Wild birds were the first to show me who I had become.

As I walked slowly along a gravel road, a dark and iridescent blue Steller's Jay floated past me, less than a foot in front of my face. Not flying, he was just gliding silently and slowly. As the air opened slightly to allow him passage, the tiniest ripple of air touched my skin.

So close! What a surprise! I wondered, "Wouldn't a wild bird feel wary being so close to a human?" Did he decide he would be safe so near me?

Some weeks later I stood on a lawn talking with a woman. In the few feet of air between us, a

Raven glided silently an inch from my face, then rose to a branch of a tree.

A month later I walked past a cherry blossom tree hearing two Chickadees chatting as they gathered their lunch. I stopped and looked up at them. They saw me and stopped talking, and their little round bodies hopped down, branch by branch, to the twig nearest me. Facing me, they stood there, gazing at me.

"Happy day!" I said to them, smiling, as they both looked at me and said hello, and I was sure they were smiling too.

Why did they interrupt their day to come and greet me, instead of ignoring me?

On a hot summer afternoon I sat down on a park bench in the shade of two large leafy trees. A Crow glided past me, less than an inch from my left cheek, then flew up and sat silently on a branch. My face still felt the barest touch of the tiny breeze created by his body in the air.

These wild birds!   Why are they behaving with such ease, such intimacy with me?

They're treating me as though I am a tree! They see me as safe!

Oh my gosh! They're telling me I have become my ideal.

I have become harmless. And Earth is showing me my truth.

~o~

Peace

At a fabric weaving cooperative just north of Cuzco, Peru, I stood laughing softly, surrounded by several gentle llamas and alpacas. Their soft wool is sheared, dyed, and woven into Peru's distinctively bright and beautiful fabrics.

The llamas and alpacas gathered around me to find out who I was, their eyes intelligent, their energy inquisitive. Smiling to their welcoming faces I was thrilled at how delightful life is.

Peru is the natural home of a bouquet of camelids. LLama and alpaca are both mostly domesticated. Vicuña have many tribes who are still wild. Guanaco, the most slender and graceful camelid in the world, are still wild. Vicuña and guanaco are slim and svelte, like ballet dancers.

The llamas and alpacas I was chatting with were friendly and sweet, happy to be enjoyed.

Out of the blue I felt an urge to look up to my

left. On the top of a little hill maybe ten feet above me stood a vicuña.

She wasn't moving and wasn't planning to move. Her face was alive with attention, and strength, and a lovely stillness. This beautiful being was looking down at me. Elegant, peaceful, she looked into my eyes and held my gaze for a long time.

When I was a girl growing up in New York City in love with the animals and the trees and the wind, did I dream in a dream I don't now remember that one day I would be sharing a long, loving gaze with a vicuña? Just us in the whole world. Eyes. Souls. Sweetness.

~o~

How To Compromise, In One Easy Lesson

On the coast of the Pacific Ocean in Washington state there's a beach which is long and smooth with sand that's comfortable to walk on. In the air and the wind is the wonderful fragrance of the sea.

If you close your eyes and just listen, you hear waves crashing near you onto the beach and you think they're much higher than they are with their strong, grown-up sound. They're only about a foot or two high, but so pretty and eager.

Standing there looking west out to where ocean meets sky, where blue meets blue, I wonder if someone in Japan is standing on a beach looking east, wondering if someone in America is looking toward them.

The first time I went to this beach I was amazed to find that you can park your car on the beach itself, right there on the sand. During weekdays, which is when I showed up, there are almost no cars around. So I drove up very slowly onto the sand to park.

Not so fast! Even though I was inside a car which therefore made me very large, I didn't own the place.

The seagulls did. Little family groups or hobby groups of six or a dozen seagulls were scattered along the beach, rummaging in the sand and talking a blue streak to each other.

When I started to drive onto the sand at almost no miles per hour, all the gulls in the nearest group looked up at my car and began explaining to the car that this patch of beach belonged to them, not to the car, and the space simply wasn't available.

They made a good point, I thought. They were here first, after all, and they seemed to like their patch of beach. I had many other choices, and why argue anyway? Arguing would just make all of us feel unhappy. And I realized that letting them have what they wanted made me feel happy for them, which made me feel happy about me.

So I backed the car up a bit and aimed it some

feet away from the gang.

When I stepped out of the car and shut the door, I looked at the gang, and said out loud to them, "Thank you, folks. Hope you're having fun today."

Four of them looked up at my face, showing their interest in me. They began to speak to me in what I can only call murmurs. No loud seagull screeches. Just quiet, gentle little gurgles that sounded like "Hi. Thanks. Have fun."

Simplicity.   Equality. Wow, isn't that relaxing? Isn't that such a nourishing way to live?

~o~

Medicine Cat

Altitude sickness! Yikes.

Today I'm at almost 10,000 feet above sea level in the Peruvian Andes, and my body is yelling at me that it doesn't like this serious lack of oxygen!

I'm obediently drinking my coca leaf tea, the millionth cup this week, to lessen the headache, the slight nausea, the weakness in my muscles, and my general feeling of reduced me-ness.

Oh what to do? Instead of sitting in this chair on the patio of the B&B, feeling all sorry for myself, I'm supposed to be climbing around Inca ruins and letting myself bathe in the cleverness and power of the ancient ways. But I don't have the strength and if I move much I'll make the headache worse. What to do?

Here comes Miss Kitty, the small brown tabby cat who lives in this B&B. She's the hostess to guests who want to chat with her, and she reminds the family who love her when it's time for her meals.

Her smart, curious face looks up at me, into my eyes, with a question in her mind, and then makes a decision. Up she jumps onto my lap, no permission requested or required.

We greet each other with smiles and loving rubs, and she curls up on my tummy and quickly goes to sleep. Oh. So much for the Inca ruins. This feels so much more nourishing.

Miss Kitty tended to me for two days, staying close while I ate just soups and drank coca leaf tea. She even visited me on the roof outside the window of my room.

She owned my lap all day for two days, bathing my body and my aura in her healing energy, her compassion and peacefulness. She was living her divine purpose, padding along her divine path, helping me raise my vibrational frequency from pretty sick to much less sick. Love and sweetness were helping to heal me.

Miss Kitty, shaman.

~O~

If Wishes Were Fishes
We'd Have Sushi For Lunch

The office manager of a company I worked for just amazed me every day. She smiled. She smiled a lot of the time, to pretty much everyone who walked into her office.

They went to her to complain about pencils, petty people, position papers. Air conditioning, heat, lighting, deadlines. Chairs, colleagues, coffee makers.

She smiled, listened attentively, engaged the folks in thinking together about possible solutions that left them both smiling.

I wondered how anyone could be so welcoming. How could anyone be so consistently warm and genuinely friendly? I *felt* friendly a lot, but I knew I didn't show it on my face very much.

How could anyone *smile* so honestly?

I wished I could be like that.

Well, why can't I?

Just because I've been serious for as long as I can remember doesn't mean I can't be something else, right? I can be whatever I decide to be, right?

Okay, how do I do that?

I could practice being what I want to be.

Practice. When I was a child and a teenager, practice practice practice was how I became really good at tying my shoelaces, climbing trees, scraping my knees.

Practice is how I got to be a performing singer. And dancer. And pianist. And a good student. And bicyclist. And swimmer. And typist.

Practice didn't work all that well with ice skating because I fell on my butt a lot. But it did work with being a writer, a photographer, a poet and a painter. Reading maps. Driving. Interviewing for jobs. Checkbook balancing.

Look at all that stuff I'm good at!

Okay, okay, I get it. It's practice. In order to

become what I want to be, I replace what I don't want to be with what I do want to be. And practice the new thing. I replace my sweet serious face with a sweet smiling face. And practice.

Can it be that easy? Why not try it? And practice it? And find out? Have I just discovered the secret of becoming who I really want to be?

I walked off to find a mirror, smiling.

~O~

Between The Sunbeams

There's a forest I know where magic dances and floats and winds through the trees, and sprites sing songs, and mushrooms the size of dinner plates wiggle with the joy of being alive. Every fallen tree becomes a nurse log, a source of food and shelter as it slowly gives its body back to the forest floor where, long ago, it was a baby sprout.

The temperate rain forest on the Olympic Peninsula in Washington state is a crowded wilderness, a world of greens and yellows and browns. The deep loamy fragrance of rich soil. Silver whispers of the leaves on the trees, the bushes and the ground. And sudden silences that echo deeper and deeper into the darkness of the forest, silences ending in the footfall of a fox or a bear, and in the conversations of eagles and thrushes.

Birds everywhere are calling to each other not to

forget something.

Tiny soft waterfalls appear, just the right size for a bird to stand and take an afternoon splash.

Three-leaf clovers are so big I could wear one as a hat!

Trees holding hands stand so close to each other I can't figure out where the faint path is, and the trees chuckle lovingly at my incompetence.

Is that a tiny purple flower moving in a little breeze? Oh wait! -- is it a faerie stopping on a leaf just long enough for me to see her, then flying off?

Why is everything so beautiful, and soft, and powerfully strong? Why is everything so visually enchanting? So emotionally and spiritually embracing?

Is this the fullness of being that ancient people would breathe in every day? Can I make my life this flourishing and gentle and beautiful?

Yes!

~O~

Communion

Her eyes took my breath away! Bright blue, looking directly into my eyes. An albino tiger with white stripes instead of orange, and dark grey stripes instead of black. And such blue blue eyes.

She sat awake and resting on the floor of her enclosure at the nation's zoo in Washington, D.C. Her sitting body seemed impossibly long. What a huge, strong being, healthy but not hunting, wise but not teaching. Looking, and seen.

This breathing treasure with the powerful face made the space in her strange life to look in my eyes, to hold my gaze, to stay with me and keep me with her, and to feel peaceful with me.

Her eyes and my eyes, together exploring, imagining. She rests in the sight of my mind always. My hand feels the warmth of her immense body. And her blue blue eyes keep looking into mine, delighting me, questioning me.

~o~

Gaia Grins

We all know that rainbows are magic. And rainbows look to me like smiles, rising in love and music from inside Earth. Gaia grinning to us.

Driving home from the grocery store I once chased a rainbow all over the Flathead Valley of northwestern Montana. I had to. The instant I saw the rainbow, it became really important to see if I could drive quickly enough to go under it and get to the other side.

Fortyish zigzag miles going north from Kalispell, the rainbow was skirting around and behind trees. An hour after I had started this chase I was approaching the dot on the map called Hungry Horse when the rainbow decided to give me the slip and slid into the forest, vanishing completely. Rats!

Arizona has vividly-colored rainbows. Maybe that's because of the very blue sky, the very beige landscape, and lots of open distance in which to watch the rainbows.

One of my most amazing rainbow experiences was in northern Alaska.

Riding in a van south from the Arctic Circle toward Fairbanks, I loved watching the wild wind move clouds all over the place. A very busy sky!

Drizzle began. Then a shower. Then sunny sky. Mother Earth wanted to keep us all guessing up on the surface.

While we were driving along the Haul Road, she sent to us a gift of glee. Rainbow after rainbow! One on the left. Here's one on the right! Hey look, just in front of us, another one! And over there! Now over here!

I counted twenty-two rainbows in less than an hour, and I was laughing so hard in delight that I gave up counting.

How sweetly Mother Earth gifted us that day, sending us grace in abundance rising all around us. How she loves us!

~O~

Angel Stuff

Total strangers. What a delight they are!

In grocery stores, with eyesight limitations I sometimes struggle to read prices or ingredients, and I'm constantly thrilled by the choices made by strangers.

A young woman will see me trying to read a product label with a magnifier, and in hesitant English will ask if she can help me. She reads aloud to me what I was looking for, and we laugh together, both of our hearts happily touching each other.

I love cut-up watermelon. Yum! But beside those small tubs of watermelon pieces on the shelf are tubs of strawberries which look the same to my odd eyesight. So I smile and ask a passing stranger if the tub I'm holding is watermelon, and the strangers always help.

I know the thing I want should be right here and

I can't find it. A couple will stop, ask, look, and find it for me, and we part with happy comments.

Out of the blue, a man will reach an arm up to grasp easily what shorter me was struggling to pull from a top shelf. While I'm thanking him in delight, usually such a person will ask if there's anything else I'd like him to find for me.

I wonder... Do these lovely people realize that they step, however briefly, into the life of someone who asks the Universe for help?

Do these lovely people realize that the Universe is giving them an opportunity to choose to be kind, and thus to express outwardly their divine beauty?

Do they know that they do the work of Angels? Do they see that they become deliverers of Love, of Light, as they live kindness and compassion? That's Angel stuff, isn't it?

As these lovely people sing their Song of grace, aren't they beautifully raising their vibrational frequency? Aren't they raising the frequency of humanity, bit by bit, and so the frequency of Earth into the frequency of divine Love?

As we accept kindness from others, aren't we lifting ourselves into a lighter, clearer, more trusting frequency, the music of divine Love?

~o~

I Choose You

There's an ancient magical tradition in Peru about Hummingbird.

In the city of Cuzco, the Incan Temple of the Sun, the Korikancha in the Quechua language, was the most sacred site of reverence to the Light, represented by the Sun.

Like many other cultures, the Inca high priests knew that only the most beautiful and the most chaste young women in the land could serve the Light. And so the only people allowed into the inner sanctum of Korikancha were these Chosen Women, the A'qlla.

Hummingbird did the selecting. Flying to a young woman, hummingbird hovered for many seconds just in front of her forehead at her Third Eye Chakra. Everyone around her therefore knew that the Light had thus chosen her as support in the temple.

When I was creating for myself a long sacred journey through Peru, I grew to know that I was one of the returning Children of The Light, a term that identifies men and women who have lived holy lives in Peru in Inca timelines.

Near Machu Picchu, I sat listening to an Andean Native young woman, my Quechua guide, explain to me the organic tea being grown on the property.

Suddenly, something flew toward my face, a Chestnut-Breasted Coronet Hummingbird. The young woman became silent and we both sat completely still.

This lovely, tiny bird came within an inch of my forehead, hovering in front of my Third Eye Chakra, looking at me as I was looking at her. I lost time. I lost breathing. The sound of her wings was all I knew, hovering, hovering.

And then she was gone.

I felt tears in my eyes. I felt blessed. I felt slightly transported into another reality, a life of love and service and light.

"Oh my goodness!" my guide said. "Do you know what that means?! I've lived in these mountains all my life and I've never before seen that happen! Do you know how important that is?"

Blessed. Beauty. Love. Light. Service. I've been chosen. In what amazing and sacred ways will my life unfold now?

~o~

Sitting Shiva

The street I lived on had lots of trees, and no sidewalks. I liked that. I could pretend I was living in the country.

Early each weekday morning I walked from my condo and pushed my way through hedges grown taller than my head. I walked along a dirt path beside the road to a street with sidewalks, to catch the bus to the office.

One April morning I saw lying at the side of the road the clean and beautiful body of a male Mallard duck. Oh golly! His body looked as though he had crossed the road and lay down, and his spirit had effortlessly left the physical. "Dear fellow," I thought, "be happy in Duck Heaven, my friend."

As I came closer I saw something else. Only a few feet away from the male Mallard's body, with hedges behind for protection sat a female Mallard, quietly looking slightly off into the distance, not speaking, not moving.

Oh my goosh! She's sitting shiva, I realized. That's the tradition in Judaism when the closest family members mourn the passing of a loved one.

Sitting shiva. This lovely lady duck was mourning her mate. My heart went out to her, and I walked way out onto the road to give them both the love and reverence they deserved.

That evening coming home from the office, there they both were, the body of the male lying in the same place at the edge of the road, and the female sitting silently in almost the same place as in the morning, facing a slightly different direction.

The next day, I went out to work, out through my hedges to the road, and there they still were. I wondered, "Am I supposed to do something? Something to help her?" I felt no idea come to me, and so I walked way out onto the road again to honor the sacredness of their privacy, and I sent love to the lady.

That evening, again, loyalty lived before my eyes. "Am I supposed to do something?" I asked her. She did not answer, and did not even look at me. So I sent love to her and pushed through my hedges to home.

The next morning, the third morning of shiva, I saw them from a slight distance and my heart was about to break. "Will she stay there until she dies? Can love really be that true?"

Walking closer I saw something new. A beautiful male Mallard duck was sitting calmly, quietly, a few feet away from the female Mallard. I knew the Universe had seen her love for her stricken mate, and had sent her someone to offer love to her. Now the two of them were sitting shiva, together.

That evening going home, as I walked past the body of the male I looked all around the area. The female Mallard who loved and the new male Mallard who had been sent by the Universe to give her a new life were nowhere to be seen.

I smiled. "Life starts again, for both of them." I looked up to the space beyond the sky and said a quick "Thank you!" to the Universe. I pushed through my hedges, smiling in happiness and belief.

~O~

Curiosity

    Seattle's wondrous zoo is close to what I imagine a magical animal forest must be.

    Everywhere are tall trees and thick bushes. Wild birds live here and squirrels who've made the zoo their territory. There are probably small wild snakes, and mice, and who knows what other beautiful beings are drawn to spend their lives and raise their families in this nourishing pretend-wilderness.

    Down a path is a busy, scurrying family of meerkats. Around this corner is a Snow Leopard watching her two little children chase a squirrel who runs up a tree and gets away. YAY!

    Every time I go to this zoo and wait in a certain spot, she appears through the trees. A Gray Wolf, the alpha female of her family, I later learned from a docent.

    She stops walking on the other side of a little forest of thin trees, turns her head toward me, and just stands there looking at me. She and I gaze at each other through the leaves and limbs, the shadows and rustles. Wolf and me. Just us.

This lovely wolf asks me questions with her eyes, and I can stroke the strength of her shoulder with my mind.

Each time, we gift to each other this sweet connection.

And I think, "I am sharing a long, gentle moment alone with a wolf! And she finds me worth her attention. Am I the luckiest person in the world!"

~O~

Living Love

My Dad was both sociable and shy, and I learned
from observing him that people who are considerate
of strangers and do nice deeds for them, often, well,
shy away from being acknowledged. That's
because, according to Dad, either they don't expect
that anyone will thank them, or their ego doesn't
need thanking, or both.

So when those kind and caring people show up,
especially on buses which are filled with strangers, I
want to acknowledge them, for their own sakes, for
my sake, and as a voice for those who did not speak,
the lines of people they've been nice to over the
years who never thanked them. I want them to
know that they are noticed, and that they deserve to
be thanked.

When I step onto a bus and swipe my fare card,
someone, often a man, unasked and quietly stands
up from one of those very front seats. As he starts

to walk to another seat, I usually have the chance to smile widely and thank him or her warmly.

Almost always their eyes light up and they smile too, and they say some variation of "You're welcome".

Seeing them light up like that always reminds me that they and I are in a transaction of Love, an exchange of our divine energy of kindness and caring.

With such simple, everyday actions we gift each other with the beauty of connection and the sweetness of optimism.

We raise our own vibrational frequency by making the softer choices.

That stranger and I are doing what we came to this planet to do, to give love, to receive love, to be love.

Even though such actions seem like little things, we are in fact changing each other's lives with goodness and grace. Isn't that marvelous?

~0~

Mr. Ibis And I

Was he as surprised as I was? He stepped out of thick, dark green bushes and trees, onto the wide paved pathway where I was walking.

He was red, brilliantly, boldly bright red. A Scarlet Ibis, he knew that he owned the ground where he walked.

He stood still when he noticed me. I stood still as soon as I noticed him. And there we stood, just a couple of feet from each other, Mr. Ibis and I.

We looked into each other's eyes. He was clearly expecting conversation. We waited for the other to begin.

"Hi," I said to him. "You are breathtakingly beautiful, and I know that you know that, but I had to tell you that and thank you for gracing me with your stunning presence.

"Look, this is your place, not mine. Please, you go first."

He did. He turned his head and calmly began walking, crossing my path right in front of me just a couple of feet away. He didn't look back at me while I stood watching this small being of soft firey feathers and quiet determination continue on his mission.

Since that day, I believe completely that when a Scarlet Ibis crosses your path, you will have bright and brilliant luck for the rest of your life!

~O~

The Hug-meister

Little Bear Lovesong, with natural eyeliner around both glacier-blue eyes, was a drop-dead gorgeous cat, and he knew it.

Complex and quiet, Little Bear was the philosopher-poet of the family. A lover of harmony in all relationships, he loved the music of Gordon Lightfoot, I think as much for the wondrous harmonies as for the body-swaying rhythms. Lightfoot's music would make Little Bear close his eyes and rock his body a bit in delight.

He and his little brother Serendipity often napped together, and when Dipity woke up he sometimes sneezed, right onto Little Bear's elegant white fur. Little Bear would go, well, catatonic, leaping to the floor to spend the next ten minutes washing and scrubbing every bit of fur contaminated by his brother's sneeze. When he finished washing, he would give us all a withering look of self-righteous indignation and walk away.

Otherwise, Little Bear was a sort of lone cowboy who spent much of each day pondering.

About twice a week, he sent me the signal. He stood in a certain spot waiting, looked at me intently, and asked, "Can we cuddle now?" My answer, of course, was always "Yes".

Little Bear walked up my belly and half sat down there. He put one arm tightly around the left side of my neck, and his other arm around the right side of my neck. Then pressing his cheek against my cheek, he sat down fully on my chest.

As I wrapped my arms around him, his silky rabbit-like fur rested on my skin. Our eyes were closed, and Little Bear began singing a love song to me, a loud, intense purr resonating against my cheek, while I sang a soft and gentle love song to him.

Holding each other in our arms. Our faces pressed together. Love, singing, heart to heart.

Love to the bone and back. Love over the moon. Love Songs.

~o~

Abundance Comes
In All Kinds Of Flavors - 1

In early January one year I had just gotten home
from over a month of a dramatic
medical adventure involving an E.R., O.R., a week in
an I.C.U., a long stay in a skilled nursing facility,
medicines, countless needles, and pain.

"Universe," I said out loud the day I was back
home, "I know a bunch of things I need and want
right now, and You know more than I do about other
things I need. So I want to create a program for
myself for this year, a schedule. Column A and
Column B.

"Column A will be opportunities for healing in
physical, emotional and spiritual ways, and for
spiritual alignment of my personality with my Higher
Self.

"Column B will be opportunities to study the
subjects I need to learn, as well as the intentional
development of my intuitive abilities. I want to train

and practice in the spiritual skills that I need to develop.

"I feel so definitely that this program is exactly what I need and want right now, so let's do this! Please guide me, Universe. Please show me what I need to see in order to live the life I truly desire. Thank you."

By doing that, out loud, clearly stating what I wanted, I was doing something I didn't realize until later: I was sending to the Universe, Source, God, Isness, a clear expression of my desire and my intention, out loud. And since my request was apparently in my highest good, magic resulted!

My first approach, for healing and alignment, was to find Reiki practitioners, to clear my body and mind and emotions, and to raise my vibrational frequency.

I did an internet search for Reiki practitioners using my zip code and made a list of names and locations. I noticed magic! The Universe had sent me many names, but three of them had first names that began with the same initial as my first name.

One even had the same first name as I do. Another had the first name I was actually born with! And one had a studio on the street where I lived.

Signs! Synchronicities! Magic!

What are the odds! ISo knew that those three people were the place to start.

In the past, I would have called all of that random "coincidence". But when I analyzed the whole list, I saw that all the other names meant nothing to me and their locations were inconvenient.

And then I knew for sure that I would never again believe in coincidence. I knew that the Universe was speaking to me through those three names, and placing a path, made just for me, in my hands. The voice of the Universe! Yes!

I laughed, and knew I had found the healers who would be in my highest good. I call that "abundance"!

Onward to the studying program!

There were two metaphysical bookstores fairly near where I lived, and I knew they had lots of classes. On their websites I found a cornucopia of classes, workshops, courses and other exciting events.

Magic again!

The Universe was dropping into my hands absolutely everything I had asked for, and more, and more!

I spent the next eleven months going to Reiki healing sessions, music concerts specifically for emotional and spiritual healing, chanting events and other healing activities, plus classes and workshops in a variety of spiritual subjects, concentrating on the topics I wanted most. I was learning about how the Universe shows up to us, and learning, in specific details, how I am a spiritual being and how that works in daily life. I call that "abundance"!

Happy as a puppy doing what I was loving, I was in those experiences two, three or even four times a week, almost every week. For eleven months! I felt that I was living a magical life. Abundance!

I learned something about abundance, and about

"prayers" being answered. I saw in real life the truth of something I learned from my first Spiritual Healer and Teacher. When wonderful things just fall into place and keep showing up for us, we can know that we are living an alignment of our conscious desires with what our Higher Self wants for us. We can know that the abundance we are receiving is proof that we're on our divine path and living in our divine purpose, whether our life looks like that to us or not at the moment.

Magic! The Universe speaking to us!

At the beginning of that year I had no idea how to align myself with the divine. That seemed like a huge unknowable thing, so I asked for help.

I simply asked Source every day to help me align more fully with my Higher Self and with my highest divine path and purpose. Every day, out loud, sincerely.

And over time I could feel the alignment growing. That's hard to describe, but I felt my thoughts and feelings about myself and others change. I felt what I said and did to myself and others change.

I became lighter, calmer, quieter, smarter,

simpler, clearer, kinder, more patient, more capable. I felt truly relaxed for the first time in my life. I felt strong, deep inside of me. I felt unafraid.

And the clue I noticed the most was that I laughed much more and much more often! That first Teacher taught me that our genuine, happy laughter raises our frequency. So when I found myself magically feeling like a goofy four-year-old child, I knew I was doing my learning well.

Laughter. Abundance? Was the Universe helping me in a way I had never thought of? Was the Universe laughing with me, kind of patting me on the head? Sweet surprise: the Universe was laughing *through* me!

~o~

Sakura

Miles of trees and masses of blossoms! Sakura, cherry blossom trees, are in full bloom every April throughout Japan.

Cherry blossom viewing is Japan's national delight, and in April all the news outlets show a map of Japan, tracking the peak blossom week as it moves from south to north.

Families pack picnic lunches on Saturdays and Sundays and go to a park or lake or a temple alive with blossoms, where they bathe in the beauty and talk about everyday things. Couples stroll, some of them hand in hand, and in the midst of such loveliness perhaps agree to spend their lives together.

The first time I experienced this peak Sakura week was in Ueno Park in the center of Tokyo, and felt instantly bewitched!

Such dense lushness of blossoms filling the air

and trees covering the ground, right inside Tokyo's busiest business area! The concentration of tall office buildings had become invisible! I could barely see the sky!

Had I slipped into a vast pale pink and white faerie garden? The tall, wide trees were crowded with blossoms, and trees crowded the sides of the walkways. Arching over the paths, the trees held hands and covered the strolling people with a gentle ecstasy of petals.

A week later I went back to Ueno Park, hoping I was still in time to swim again in that delicate loveliness.

A breeze at my back urged me on as I entered the park.

I walked onto a new carpet of petals.

Turning in all directions I was seeing only loose little blossoms bouncing in the air, filling the air. Diaphanous. Dizzying.

I had stepped into a poem.

White snow and pink snow

fluttering and floating
gracing my hair,
blessing my face,
kissing my upraised open hands,
 Sakura Faerie painting the world,
brown branches, blue sky
near hidden from sight,
I dance in meanders
your flower-snow Song.

~o~

Auburn And Caramel

At a comfy B&B where I stayed for a few days in Calca in the Sacred Valley of Peru, some of the recurring visitors were hummingbirds feasting on nectar, some were morning clouds resting against the mountainside into which the house had been built.

Two of the permanent residents were chickens. They lived in a very large enclosed courtyard with trees and flowers and lots of grassy exploring space where they could find bits of this and specks of that.

One chicken was a light caramel color and the other a deep, shining auburn. They spent most of their days meandering oh-so-slowly in the grass, pecking pecking pecking, busy, focused on making their living.

I noticed something special about them. Auburn was never more than a couple of steps from Caramel, looking at Caramel every several seconds. Caramel seemed content to always have Auburn at her side.

I mentioned to the woman who owned the B&B that the two chickens seemed to be good friends and asked if Auburn was maybe taking care of Caramel in some way.

"Yes. She's in love with Caramel," said the woman.

"Oh I'm so happy that she loves," I said. "Love is the best thing in life, isn't it? Thank you for telling me. And does Caramel love her too?"

"I don't know," said the woman. "This is the first time I've lived with a gay chicken, so I don't know how to figure that out."

From then on, I enjoyed watching Auburn and Caramel live their lives slowly together, always near each other, never apart. They frequently spoke very softly to each other. Their tiny murmurs filled the air around them with attentiveness and peacefulness.

I realized that it didn't matter if I figured out their relationship. *They* had figured it out, lovingly, gently, and that's all that mattered.

~O~

Grace

Strolling in a woodsy aviary in Florida I turned a corner to see a very tall, huge birdcage. My eyes were about level with the tips of the tails of two birds, and I moved my eyes up and up those very long tails to find the faces of the birds.

I looked into the eyes of two magnificent Hyacinth Macaws. The largest parrot in the world, the Hyacinth is strange, mysteriously beautiful, formed in the richness of the hyacinth color, radiating grace and intelligence and wisdom.

The two amazing Hyacinths were sitting quietly shoulder to shoulder on their perch., gazing down at me.

For a timeless time, maybe even a couple of minutes, we three stayed together, being together, enjoying together, lifting each other up, silently, in love. I remember their eyes and their beauty so vividly...

Many years later, I took a guided shamanic journey simply to say hello to my Power Animals. My highest intention for the journey was to thank them for their love and guidance and giggles.

They had a surprise and a gift for me.

They brought in a Hyacinth Macaw as my new Guide, someone who would be a new Power Animal for me, who would be with me, helping me, for a very long time.

He's an imaginative and merry being with a wonderfully goofy sense of humor.

He has turned out to be a wordy bird as most parrots are, with a lot to say much of the time. So he helps me to write, especially about animals and birds and the natural world. He sends, through me, the Songs they want to sing to the world.

His feathers are so soft, and his eyes are always laughing, as he lives his divine purpose scattering grace and singing his own Song to us all.

~o~

Coyote Rainbow

Somewhere in northwestern Arizona I drove my old black van to the side of the road to eat a sandwich. The air was hot and dry and still.

As I ate and looked into the vast blue sky, I thought I saw something move on the other side of the narrow road. I focused.

A wolf? I don't think so, not here. A dog? Walks oddly for a dog. The animal was lithe, certain and at attention, constantly looking around. Of course! A coyote! The first I'd ever seen.

I watched this interesting being lope along, apparently knowing exactly where he was going.

Did he just glance at me for more than a moment? "Wow!" thought the back-east big-city girl in me. And the coyote quickly loped up the road out of sight.

Soon I drove back onto the road in the same direction as the coyote, to see more of Arizona.

The sky quickly grew gray, then darker gray, then extremnely dark gray. I wondered, "Am I driving to the end of the world?"

Suddenly, a rainbow! So vivid against the gray. So clear it was almost ringing and lightly reverberating in high-pitched tones!

As I drove slowly, Ooh! a second rainbow, above the first! Two glorious arches of singing light, together, right in front of me!

Where's the rain? Isn't there supposed to be rain to make rainbows? All I heard was my van's engine, so I pulled over and turned it off.

Silence.

And when I looked up into the dark gray sky, there were *three* rainbows! Floating together like vibrating, humming lights moving in harmony toward the heavens. My eyes filled with tears. Who, in all their life, ever sees a triple rainbow? Me! Me!

I called out, "Coyote! Do you see this?! Do you love this? Did you give this to me? Thank you, Spirits of this land! I will treasure your gift forever."

~O~

Eclipse Epiphany

On August 21, 2017 all across America from sea to shining sea, the Earth and all who lived on her experienced a total eclipse of the Sun by the New Moon in Leo. Archangels and astrologers alike had forecast this eclipse as a monumentally transformational event in the history of Earth and all humanity.

Before the hour, I gathered some of my crystal and stone friends. Moldavite, Shattukite, Kunzite and Lemurian Seed Quartz pendants, and other jewelry of Azurite, Malachite, Rose Tourmaline, Iolite, Tanzanite and Amethyst. They and I had some wondrous spiritual and healing experiences.

We went outside at 9:00 in the morning to walk and taste the world, and then find a tree who wanted us to be with her for the big moment at 10:20.

It was party day in the Pacific Northwest! Normally empty sidewalks were peppered with people in little groups and larger groups, strolling, meandering, watching, young people and old people, middlers, children and assorted dogs.

Everyone was smiling or laughing including the dogs. They talked with each other, obviously delighted to share their excitement. They leaned in closer to each other than people in public usually do.

Folks reached out with cardboard viewing glasses in their hands, offering a look to strangers walking by. Sharing their cardboard glasses back and forth with each other, they looked directly at the Sun, doing something so forbidden and magical and not being struck dead.

Two or three heads were close together facing away from the Sun . They looked at their pinholed papers, and watched, backwards, as the Moon moved across the Sun. They oohed and ahhed and laughed, and in their excitement they all talked at the same time.

Complete strangers began long conversations, discovering they both loved to play softball or power-walk in the mornings, or used to live in Argentina, or are able to do math in their head and don't understand why everyone doesn't do that.

Were these the same people who usually didn't seem even to notice that others exist? Today they were amazed together, enthusiastic together. They had become happy, open, welcoming each other and life to come into their hearts.

This is better than recess! This is like being let out early from school!

Becoming sudden playmates, they were actively bringing light to the shadow of not knowing. Light, love, laughter were eclipsing habits of controlled attitudes and behaviors.

"Universe, we should do this more often," I thought. "Look at how much fun everyone's having! And how easily they love when they've raised their vibration like this, laughing and loving life."

My crystals and I met a tree who wanted us to be with her. Under the cloudless blue sky and the summer warmth of the Sun, together the tree and the crystals and I stood and waited for the big moment at 10:20.

I think I expected some sort of medieval darkness in day, with neighborhood animals wailing in confusion and birds going home asking each other why they ate so little that day.

In the Seattle, Washington area we had a 92% eclipsing of the Sun by the Moon. It cooled the morning quite a bit, and erased most of the shadows of trees and buildings, and made the day a little darker. But no medieval mystery.

I and my crystals and friend tree stood unhidden, greeting the energies that were changing the world.

I thought a new thought. "I can absorb the change that is happening in the cosmos. I can take in the newness. I can become a me I don't yet know."

Everyone watching and paying attention, and everyone not watching and not paying attention, became bathed in the MoonSunLight, a new light.

All living beings including Earth became part of

the Universe living Its own symbolism as the great
round shadow was brought to face fully the great
round light. They slow-danced together and talked
with each other, that shadow Moon and that light
Sun, as they looked fully into each other.

Every eclipse is a sweet gift from the Universe,
because its energies bring to a close those aspects
of ourselves and our lives which no longer serve us.
And the eclipse energies open the windows of our
lives, and of our understanding of ourselves, to bring
in the new circumstances and insights that will
nourish us now on our path of spiritual development.

People began, that day, trying something new.
They began changing their lives, one smile at a time,
one feeling of delight at a time, one sharing at a
time, bringing divine healing and love to themselves
and each other, and to their planet. Collective
consciousness rising.

Somewhere deep inside, humanity called out that
day, "Universe, bring it on! I can absorb this! I am,
therefore I become."

~O~

Play With Me?

At a sprawling ranch in Washington state, summer evening light lasts until close to 10:00 at night. I sat idly on a well-worn wooden bench on the large porch, watching the hummingbirds crowd around the red feeder, getting their millionth meal of the day.

One female hummingbird flew toward me, hovered for an instant in front of my face, then flew around my head slowly, close to me.

She stopped at my forehead. Then she flew slowly all around my head again. Forehead stop. Around again.

I sat, not moving, not breathing, transfixed with joy to be the object of attention of this tiny, magical being.

She stopped again and hovered in front of my face.

"Are you a flower?" she asked me. "If you are,

why are you shaped so oddly? If you're not, will you play with me?"

Then she was gone, back to the red feeder, back to her regular life. And in my regular life I could keep in my heart a sweet invitation on a warm summer evening.

~o~

Ahhh, Bake!

"Hey, I haven't seen you here in a while. Welcome back!"

"Thanks. I tried out a different spot for sun-bathing, but this place is better."

"Did you go out of Tokyo?"

"No, just stayed in town."

"Did the place have a great surface to grab onto like this stucco wall?"

"No, it was a beautiful traditional Japanese house. The outside walls were wonderfully fragrant wood , but they were a bit difficult to hold onto."

"Wood, huh? I've always wondered what that would be like to cling to. Not easy?"

"Not for me. But you're a larger lizard than I am so it might work for you."

"Yeah, but wood's dark. This white stucco soaks

up the morning sunshine so it warms my belly while the sun warms my back."

"Man does this feel warm! I feel that I'm coming back to life after sleeping all night."

"Did you hear that?"

"What?"

"A door closing. Yep, she's locking it now. She'll be walking by in a minute."

"Wait a second, I want to set my tail into a sexy curl and look super handsome for her. I've missed seeing her. I think she really liked me."

"Oh c'mon, I'm better looking than you, and bigger. And my grey scales are brightening up just right in this hot morning sun. Hey! Here she is."

A young woman walks onto the grass beside the house. She looks up and smiles to the two little grey lizards stretched out in the sunshine.

"'Hi, fellas," she says. "You look so pretty this morning."

She points to the carefully curled tail. "And wow, look at your tail! You look elegant. You're both doing such a good job of holding up the side of the house! Take good care of it today. Bye." And she turns and walks away.

"I can't understand a word she says, can you?"

"Well she's not speaking in Japanese, that's for sure. But she seems nice, doesn't she?"

"Yeah, friendly. Did you hear that? She said I look elegant!"

"But I'm still bigger than you ."

"Yeah, but I'm handsomer. She li-i-i-ikes me!"

~O~

Why Doesn't My Brain Grow Bigger?

Shouldn't it?

All those years!Multiplication tables. The Periodic
Table. "I before E except after C." The differences
among homonyms like way, weigh and whey. Sea
or ocean? French horn or marching horn? Nook, or
cranny?

Blizzards of passwords, phone numbers, birth
dates, street addresses.

And all those names! People, pets, cars, streets,
towns, book titles, movie titles, songs, brands, ice
cream flavors, dog breeds.

How many feet are in a meter? How many Great
Lakes are there? How far is it to the moon? How
many shades of blue-green are there? I can think of
teal, peacock, turquoise, aqua, Chivor emeralds.

My brain never grows to keep on filing all this
stuff? That doesn't make sense! Why?

What if my brain does my body work like

circulation, and my organizing work like vacation planning?

What if there's something much larger, a source of information from which my brain simply grabs things when I want the information?

I'm thinking of a flower. I'm trying to remember the name of the flower. All around the world millions of people are trying to remember the name of a flower. Does every single person in the whole entire world have to store all the names of flowers? Wouldn't Nature, exemplar of efficiency, consider all that multiplication of effort inefficient? Even indecent?

Instead, wouldn't a central storehouse of flower names from which we all can extract the name we want, be efficient?

What if there is a larger consciousness, call it, say, Universal Consciousness or Cosmic Consciousness or the Akashic Records, which contains all information, everything that has ever been known, is now known, and will ever be known? What if *that's* where the electromagnetic zaps of our brains go when we're trying to recall the name of a flower? And what if the zap reels in the name to our brain like an electromagnetic fishing line?

What if this central storehouse has just one original that can be copied infinitely, instead of having those millions of originals in Earth brains?

Does my brain not grow bigger because it doesn't have to store any of this stuff because all that work is already done for me?

And wouldn't the information in such a storehouse therefore be limitless?

And wouldn't I be able to access anything, everything, all through time, all before time, all after time, in all Creation? Isn't that what, in part, meditation is for? And, ultimately, isn't that what thinking and daydreaming and imagining are for, at least partially?

Doesn't that mean that infinity is always right at my fingertips? And that I'm actually living in eternity?

~0~

Rain, My Love

I hear the distant muffled crashes and slow deep rumbles behind the clouds who are watching everything.

My nose is drawing in the fragrances of wet soil and sodden tree bark.

My tongue wants to taste the heavy air thick with the scent of soil and the transforming fragrance of the sacred Western Red Cedar. I breathe I breathe I breathe in, blessing my body with the grace of those aromas.

Grasses bend, holding on their backs the weight of raindrops. Into the deep, dark crevices in tree bark other raindrops run and hide from the thunder.

Trees, do any of you want to go in out of the rain?

I hear the voices of the birds who are telling rain stories to each other, as they flutter their feathers and fling raindrops into the air to splash into drops coming down from the clouds.

I hear the tiny staccato dance of raindrops on the leaves, on the soil, on my coat.

Rain! Oh rain, my love!

I am wet, washed, drenched, my clothes dripping. You carress my hair. I raise my face to you, and shake you from the feathers of my hair.

Oh rain, you touch my face. I feel you kiss my forehead, my eyelids, my cheeks, my lips. Drips slip in at the corners of my mouth, and on the edges of my tongue taste clean and free like air.

You hold my hands in yours, sweet rain. You bathe me, you cover me, you saturate me, in love.

I become an Earth being, at home in you.

~0~

Be This Me

"Is there a task I could do to help you?" I asked the owner of a sprawling ranch where I was staying for a couple of nights, on the Olympic Peninsula in Washington state.

"I'd really like to do something." Some of my childhood was spent on a farm and I figured I could be useful to the B&B ranch owner.

"Would you like to feed the goats?" she asked. I was thrilled!

Goats! Yippee! I love goats.

"Before we get their feed, you need to understand that the goats belong to the dogs. The dogs manage the herd, so before they will allow you to have any contact with the goats, you must pass their inspection. Do you understand?"

Goats *and* dogs! Double yippee! So this is why I came to this ranch, so that I could feel so happy.

I held the large tray of feed carefully as I

followed instructions to open the gate in the first fence, close it and lock it behind me, then open the gate in the second fence, close it and lock it, and then stand still waiting for the verdict from the dogs.

And then I saw them. Three dogs. One stayed many yards back with the goats who also stood, watching and waiting. And two dogs calmly walked to me. Large, all-white Great Pyrenees dogs. Such beautiful dogs, with serene faces like Angels, intelligent, calm and ethereal eyes, deliberate manner, powerful bodies. They radiated curiosity and ownership.

I opened my free hand and slowly extended it for them to smell, as they focused on my eyes. And for the first time in my life I met dogs with stars in their eyes. I was instantly in love, and had almost forgotten I had come here for the goats.

The silent signal was broadcast, and most of the fifteen or so goats walked to me quickly. They were in all sizes and colors, and stood around me munching the feed while the two dogs stood around them watching.

None of us spoke. We all moved slowly, gently,

feeling relaxed together. Trust. Happiness. Right living.

I stood surrounded by goat intelligence and merriness, and dog intelligence and confidence.

I stood bathing in the love between the goats and the dogs, and between me and all of them.

I stood feeling the sweetness and simplicity of all their acceptance of me.

I stood knowing how safe we all felt together, how comfortable we all knew we were together.

My heart called out "Stay! Stay. Be this me, this gentle centerdness, this joyous powerfulness, this love, this softly flowing oneness. Be this me for now and always."

~o~

Changing Beliefs, Changing Expectations

What happens when a man walks through his own portal? -- the portal that he himself imaged before he came forth to this incarnation, knowing that this time, at long last, he would be lightning and magics, and would build the cosmic and etheric and human powers to create the portal, and to use it...

What happens when he walks from what he knew to what is brand new?

What happens when Source expressing as that man, and thus they are being united intention -- what happens when, loving to take risks because he is Source and that's what Source does, the man turns risk-taking into judiciously free and wild creativity, generative creativity, magnificently beautiful creativity?

What happens when we let go, and let new?

Worlds begin...

~O~

Learning The Song

Change
and become like little children.
- Matthew 18:3

Empathy

I spent today in a forest.
Dark, damp, deliciously chilly. My perfect weather!
"Well then, I must be a mushroom," Alice exclaimed.

~o~

Dance In The Sky

White walking on white. The huge Polar Bear, one of the tribes who own and roam far northern Alaska and Canada, is deep into his first winter alone and independent. He steps crunch after crunch in the new snow.

He knows this trail well, worn into the ice by the weight of his own graceful and powerful body over the dark months of autumn and winter. He's off to catch dinner at one of his favorite dark-weather dinner-catching spots.

His large hands and feet crush small spaces into the vast snowland above the ice. Looking straight ahead into a horizon beyond reach, he contemplates the nature of darkness, the changing reality of darkness, the lush beauty of darkness. He knows well a life of darkness all around and whiteness all below.

As he walks that familiar path, out of the blue he has an unfamiliar idea, to turn just a bit away from the trail. As he does, he sees a different part of the darkness.

His heart skips a beat in joy and wonder, and he stops walking and looks up.

The sky is alive!

Blues and greens are floating across the darkness in waves and streams and ribbons. Now a light blue! Now an almost-white. Ah! There's a vivid green, much lighter than the tiny leaves in the summer tundra.

A wave now of very blue. And there a green and a blue seem to melt into each other, a new color. Comes a whie ribbon. Comes a green.

Staring up into the dancing sky, the Polar Bear who never expected to have his life interrupted, wonders what these colors are called. He remembers his mom telling him about when the sky dances, and he remembers seeing this sometimes when he was younger. But this is the first time he's seen such deep colors, such busy waves and streams. He wonders if his mom ever told him the name of this dance, or if he just doesn't remember.

He thinks that maybe, then, he can give it a name of his own.

He wonders if he stops looking will the colors stop? He can see the stars behind the streams and in between the ribbons. Is this what the darkness always does when he is looking the other way?

Are these floating colors the oceans and rivers of the sky? Are they messages from the stars? Are they pathways that the stars send out, so that they can ride down to meet him?

His tummy tells him he wants to eat, and he considers where to go. The old path leads to food but offers only darkness. This new path leads to surprise and the unexpected, but offers such delight he finds that he does not want to resist the joy.

So he walks on this new path that he's making with each step. Half watching where he walks, half gazing up into the dance, he walks toward the magic.

He wonders on this new, beautiful path will he walk onto a green or blue or white ribbon and up into a star?

~O~

Cosmic Complaint Department

Reply

Yes, We hear you. We understand that you do not like the many situations, people, foods, jeans, prices, weather that you frequently complain about.

PLACING AN ORDER
We request the following information. What do you actually *want*? When you tell Us clearly what you *do* want, We are more able to fill your order. Use as much detail as you wish, bearing in mind, of course, that details are always subject to change within the constantly-changing conditions of the Universe.

BEST METHOD
In fact, your most successful course of action

would be to state clearly how you want to *feel* when you receive your order, rather than details about the order itself.

When you practice feeling the way you want to feel, and then describe that feeling in words, you may leave the details to Us, because We know exactly what will fulfill you the most.

We recommend, therefore, that you carve out a bit of time, say ten minutes, each day to place your order(s), using words that create as definite a feeling as you can.

CHANGES

If at any time you decide you want to change your order, just refer to your previous order on the same subject, and state your changes. We have a perfect filing system and can instantly make the changes you request.

SECRET SAUCE

Be sure to speak your orders and changes out

loud in a confident, calm voice. This will tell Us that you mean what you say and your request is not a momentary random thought. The more happy expectation, excitement, even joy, with which you speak your desires, the more We will believe that your request is serious.

We deeply appreciate working with you.

Fulfillment is Our business.

~o~

Thunder Blessing

At 11:00 at night, I snuggled into a comfy twin bed in a delightful little house, a B&B's *casita,* in Urubamba, Peru, at the northern end of the Sacred Valley.

Yawn, yawn. I was sleepy from a bit of altitude sickness and a lot of wondrous experiences in and near Machu Picchu.

In a beautiful shamanic *despacho* ceremony the previous day, I had offered my greetings and gratitude to the Spirits of the place, the area and the holy mountains. My merry Shaman, who conducted the ceremony, was the steward of the holiest mountain of the Andes.

We were assisted by a hummingbird who sat quietly on a branch just inches from my back for an amazing twenty minutes, a rest that hummingbirds almost never take. As I blessed the mountain, the bird blessed me.

Being in the lush, thick "cloud forest" way up in the Andes was a constant thrill. I kept feeling great surges of delight at seeing Andean and Amazonian birds I'd never known. And I kept meeting new people, playing and learning with them as we shared our surprises and discoveries.

Yawn... I love my life...

Crash!! The thunder was right outside my window, the loudest I had ever heard.

I awoke instantly, *smiling*, feeling happy, pleased and relaxed. I knew absolutely in my whole being that the Thunder Spirit was saying to me, "WELL DONE!!"

I glanced at my clock. It was 1:30 in the morning. Rain was pouring outside.

I grinned and said thank you to the Thunder Spirit. I closed my eyes, and wrapped myself in my joy and the powerful embrace of that mighty blessing, and slipped back into sleep.

~O~

Discernment

Walking to the bus in the mornings on my way to work, I always passed between two long rows of very tall hedges, thick and leafy.

The hedges on my left were worked by a gaggle of Chickadees chatting busily as they hunted for breakfast.

The row on my right always hid quiet Crows.

One Crow was the lookout, and he and I often exchanged glances as I walked past him.

One day I stopped, looked at him looking at me, and asked, "Do *we* all look alike to you, too? Or are you more discerning than we are?"

He moved his head just a bit. Was that a little nod? Given the complex intelligence and creativity of crows, was he suggesting that I try to find him in a crowd of crows, and he try to find me in a crowd of humans, and see who wins?

~o~

Calling In The Ancestors

In their love for us, in their open hands, our ancestors gave us everything they were.

In our DNA we carry their dreams and happiness, their fears and failures, their wisdom and wonderings and wanderings. We are more than that, of course, but we are definitely what they became and so what they gave us of themselves, to give us a start in becoming ourselves.

We also carry in our DNA their memories of their ancestors who roamed the mountains and the plains, sailed the waters, and were the pioneers with fire and spears, language and art and invention.

We are connected, deeply, through the ages, to what they tried and to their triumphs and sorrows. We don't have to imitate them, but we have to know what we have come from. That helps us to know what we can make of ourselves, and why we want to do that.

I am the result of three lines of Celts, originally marauders through Europe. Centuries later after settling in Ireland, some of their descendants were among the 9th Century kings of Wicklow and others were from Brian Boru in Tipperary, the 10th Century king of all Ireland.

Over time, after being invaded by the Vikings and then forcibly driven from their lands by the English, they became the guardians, for all the western world, of knowledge, art and elegant language. My personal belief is that the highly spiritual beings who lived on the island of Hy-Breasal, west of Ireland, had something to do with this Irish devotion to beauty, and maybe someday I'll be able to prove that.

Eventually my ancestors became calm respected farmers and merchants. They replaced their ancient heritage of conquering violence with political and religious vehemence.

They lived mysticism and magic dripping from their poetry and tall tales and daily expectations. Story-telling. The "gift of gab". Deep-seated victim consciousness and anger. Profound, loving communion with the soil, green growing things and animals, and with the Little People. One of my grandmothers, an immigrant to America from Ireland at age 19, told me that as a little girl on the farm she often put out a saucer of milk at night for the Little People, and in the morning the milk was always gone so she knew the Little People had enjoyed it.

Pillage and plunder inflicted long ago. Pillage and plunder received not so long ago. Deprivation. Displacement. Desperation. Deliverance into new lives in new lands.

Endurance, patience, vast courage, imagination, hope. Trust in the Divine.

I am also the result of one line of Hebrews who long, long ago wandered from the Middle East into Egypt and then Morocco and into southern Spain.

They lived lives of the well-educated, becoming over time honored teachers, revered rabbis and respected tradespeople. They were passionate about deep intellectual explorations of all topics under the sun, and about endless discussion together, lively, discovering, learning, teaching, delighting in knowledge for its own thrilling sake.

They, too, had the "gift of gab".

In general they lived comfortable lives, until confronted by the hell of the Spanish Inquisition. In desperation, they chose life, survival and cleverness as pretend-converts to Catholicism over torture and death as Jewish martyrs. And centuries later, once again one chose a new life in a new land.

Endurance, patience, vast courage, imagination, hope. Trust in the Divine.

Today our ancestors watch us and cheer us on, smiling with us in our successes, weeping with us in our woundings.

Our ancestors love us.

They ask us for our forgiveness for what they could not teach us because they did not know.

They ask us for our understanding and compassion for what they could not give us, because they had not yet become that.

They ask us for our pride in what they were, to match their pride in who we have become.

In their loving open hands our ancestors gave us

everything they were.

By calling them to us now, out loud in the secrecy of our home, we can at last thank all the generations of them for their gifts to us. We can offer to them, out loud, our forgiveness, our understanding, our compassion and our pride.

In doing this we can heal their sins against themselves, and heal any burdens we have carried about them. We can release that karmic baggage, for ourselves and for them.

We will free ourselves from a near and ancient legacy, and so free ourselves to fly, over the mountains, through the plains, across the waters, into the dreams we have for ourselves.

Love heals everything. Love frees everything.

~o~

A River Rumbles, A River Roars

I felt pulled into history, driving south from Seattle, Washington in my big old van pulling my travel trailer.

I was on a wide highway that used to be a narrower wagon trail, that used to be a First People's walking trail, that used to be a deer trail, that was born as a bed scraped out and shaped by glaciers that were, like me, just passing through.

To go from Blythe, California into Arizona, I faced a bridge over the mighty and historic Colorado River. In honor of this grand giver of life and shaper of the land, I pulled over and stepped out to go meet this powerful being for the first time.

Dark blue he was, full with Spring snowmelt, quiet. Running, running, running in a deep, heavy, low rumble. Muscular, intense. Brawny shoulders down, charging ahead, pushing ahead, determined and serious.

I wondered if he remembered how he used to

be, before all the dams were built upstream, when he was free and flying. He was so quiet and serious now. I wondered if he would even hear such a question, if I asked him...

Many years later , I rode in a slow train on a single set of tracks hugging the side of the Andes Mountains in Peru. From Ollantaytambo to Aguas Calientes, a short distance from Machu Picchu, the amazing 1920s feat of engineering ran in a narrow cut of land between the mountainside and the Urubamba River.

He was brown with the nourishing silt that he carried downstream, all the way to the Amazon River. The Urubamba knew nothing of dams. Noisy, free and wild, he was leaping, dancing and twirling at every rock, every bend.

Urubamba played every chance he got, tossing bits of foam and silt in all directions, a swirling, roiling partner with all he passed.

Does the Colorado remember when he was like the Urubamba, merry and primal? Does he miss that? Does he forgive?

~0~

One More Mindful Step

What is *really* in my best interests? What will *nourish* me, and maintain my state of happiness? And what will, at the same time, nourish others?

When I was in college I wanted to spend my money on books and on beer with my friends, so I taught myself how to cut, style and color my hair, which gave me more money and more time. Sweet!

I developed a short, layered hair style that I really have loved over the years, and I grew proud o f this skill. Double sweet!

Some years ago I was in a sort-of nursing home getting physical therapy. The facility housed a tiny hair salon with just one chair. Once or twice a week a woman took care of customers who lived in the nursing home.

I decided to treat myself and let someone else do my hair for the first time in decades. In the chair, I described to the lady with the scissors what I wanted and she said that she understood.

A half-hour later I discovered that I now had almost less hair than I did as an infant. Ooops!

I love the Universe. It's always giving us opportunities to become more than we were a minute ago. And hair does grow back.

Regardless of what I say and do, regardless of how kind and warm I may appear to be to others, what I'm actually feeling on the inside is what tells me who I really am right now. My emotional reactions are me. And feelings are always choices, so I always have the golden gift of choosing to be who I like or who I could like better, who I truly admire or who I don't admire.

ARRGGH, I thought beneath the tiny haircut. I'll bet I look like a boy. I don't want to look like a boy.

Well waitaminute. People will be so delighted being in my company, and so completely uninterested in anyone's hair except their own, that they'll never get past my eyes and my smile, right? Anyway, that's what my mother used to tell me when I was a teenager. And my hair is so short I won't have to think about it for at least three months. Yay!

Smiling, and feeling happy, I tipped the woman well, and touched her arm when I thanked her warmly.

Catching a glimpse of me in a mirror as I walked out of the salon, I smiled at me, knowing that by choosing kindness and happiness I had just taken one more step up and away from anger, one more step into the Light, loving myself and giving myself, others and Earth the best me I can be. Way to go, me!

~o~

Raun, Intimate Stranger

After the sun goes down in Peru, when the darkness changes the world to secrets, I discovered something I had not known and could not see, could only hear.

After the sun goes down, the dogs owned the neighborhoods.

After dark, the dogs came out to live their lives in public.

They walked alone or in small groups of friends, with no humans in sight, calling to one another. "Marco!" "Polo!"

"Wait up!"

"Miguel, where are you?"

"Anyone seen Rodrigo?"

"Marissa, where did Alejandro go?"

Turns out that the names they call themselves are quite elegant.

One evening I arrived at a B&B and was greeted by the wife and husband owners, one large white and grey dog who looked like an Akita, and another dog, all brown and smooth, the size of a small pony.

He was introduced to me as Raun, a Great Dane and Mastiff mix, and with me standing on two feet and him on four our eyes were almost level. What a surprise!

Raun decided to walk to me. I offered him my open hand and he examined it. He moved toward me and gently leaned half his body weight against me. I scritched up and down his side. The wife laughed and warned me that now Raun would never leave me!

Raun walked behind me and the owners to my *casita*, a little house, where he sat down and waited on the patio as darkness completed. After many minutes I went out of the *casita* and said his name softly, and we walked to each other.

I don't know how long we spent together that evening. Maybe a half-hour. Time vanished. I scritched his head, his neck, his chest, his sides, until he moved his body a bit so I'd scritch a new spot.

I felt his complete contentment in receiving a gift he dearly loved. And I felt my own complete contentment in having an important job and doing it mindfully, with love. Raun was humming in his heart, and I was humming in mine. Neither of us said a word. Such sweetness, such simplicity, so much shared love.

A short bark sounded off in the distance, rising out of the darkness. Raun spoke only one syllable in response toward the darkness.

He turned his head and looked his thanks to me, and quickly walked off, disappearing into the night where the dogs of Peru reign.

~O~

A Hero's Journey

A small yellow butterfly was working hard to free herself when I walked past the window. She had been absent from Physics class the day the teacher explained windows. Her mom had kept her home from school because she was sneezing. So she didn't know that the window was not a portal to the world.

"Why me, God?" I asked, knowing I had never touched a butterfly and didn't know how to do it. "Why did all the forces of the Universe put me in this place in this moment, giving me the choice to rescue her, or not?"

"Watch her, and she will tell you how to hold her," was the answer inside me.

I watched. She worked hard to escape to a world she could see and believe in. She fluttered her wings for some seconds as she pushed her tiny but strong body against the window pane to get through it. If intention and will and bodily strength by themselves could have moved or melted the glass, she would have freed herself.

Then she stopped. She closed her wings flat together, not moving at all. She spent some seconds catching her breath, resting her wings and gathering determination.

Flutter. Close. Flutter. Close. Then I knew what to do.

Flutter. Close. Carefully, quickly I put my thumb and middle finger on either side of her closed wings and grasped, gently and firmly.

Instantly all through her wings muscles tightened! Muscles? Their wings have muscles? I never knew! Stop thinking and take her out into the world!

I was walking in my life holding a small yellow butterfly who was pushing all her muscles against me in one of the strangest sensations I'd ever felt. I quickly found a nice bush, placed my hand on a leaf, and opened my fingers, which suddenly felt free, free from protest.

The small yellow butterfly staggered slightly for a

step or two, fluttered her wings a bit, and I'm certain looked around to figure out where she was. She walked on the leaf, and then flew off into the rest of her life.

When she gets home, will the ones who love her rejoice at her return? Will they sing and dance? What will she tell them about her adventure? Will she tell the story of the giant who captured her? Will she tell of her courage and then her joy?

Will she help others understand the nature of windows? Will she help them understand that benevolence exists and help comes when we need it?

Will she show others the way by teaching them that we really can trust the Universe to have our back, to send us what we need?

If she does, if she passes along her new wisdom, she will change the world.

~o~

Abundance Comes
In All Kinds Of Flavors - 2

Why can't people be the way I want them to be?

You know, those people who don't return phone calls or answer questions or emails. And those people who are usually late, or interrupt me while I'm talking, or forget when my birthday is, or never seem to be able to pay their share, or who quickly criticize anything.

Sometimes I get angry about them. Why can't they be more congenial?

Why can't people be the way I want them to be?!

Thinking about this one day I remembered that a Spiritual Teacher taught me to see differently. Look at things differently from the way I usually look.

Change *how I see*, in order to change how I feel. Wow!

But why would I want to change me?

Because I can't change anyone else. No one can

change anyone. So I can't "fix" anyone.

And I take me and my reactions wherever I go, all the time. So if I change the way I see things and thus change my reactions, I can feel happier everywhere, anytime. Not to ignore what happens, but to go higher. To go Lighter.

Because this is my life and I want to live it in relaxation, not annoyance.

See differently. How would I do that?

Well, see that people are not exactly their behavior. People's words and actions express only how they are in that moment.

Everyone is always doing the best they can at any time in any situation. And if I judge someone for being judgmental, won't I be holding onto what I want to release?

I don't know what personal history has led them to be who they are in a given moment. I don't know what they are struggling with in their minds, in their hearts, in their karma.

Instead, I can look at people through the eyes of Source, Who knows that everyone is beautiful and fine in their essence, and that they are doing the best they can in the moment.

See *divinely*. That's it!

Relax. Forgive. Let go. See higher.

This is going to take practice, I think, to see people as beautiful and fine no matter what their words or actions may be. Okay, I can do practice.

If my reward to myself is relaxing, forgiving, letting go, and smiling inside and out, I absolutely can practice seeing people as divine, as essentially beautiful and fine.

Okay, life! I want to practice!

I want to see each person I encounter as a gift to me, a golden opportunity to look at them through the mind of God and see them as God sees them, divinely created beauty.

So if they don't show up on time, I will know that the Universe is gifting me with the abundance of an opportunity to be calm, forgiving, relaxed and loving. Loving to them. Loving to me. Win, and win.

I like this idea!

~O~

How To Forgive,
In One Easy Lesson

My first cat, Tammy, wore a brown tabby coat with small black stripes, a white throat and white hands and feet. Very pretty. And she had very intelligent amber eyes.

I was a high school teacher at the time and often took students' papers home to read and grade. Tammy loved to help me, sitting close to my side, offering comments and suggestions.

Reading reports one day, I stood up from our place on the sofa and went to the kitchen to get grapes. When I got back to the sofa where I had placed the thin pile of papers, I saw that wet bits of paper were all over the floor and the sofa. A corner of the papers was pretty much chewed away.

Having little wisdom then, and thinking the chewed corners actually mattered, I was furious and yelled at Tammy a few loud sentences of my unenlightened opinion.

Tammy wisely jumped to the floor and hid under the other end of the sofa.

Fuming, I cleaned up the mess, sat down, and angrily got back to grading the papers.

Minutes passed in silence.

Then from under the sofa beside my foot, Tammy's face appeared looking up at me. I looked at her quietly, and her body emerged and turned toward me.

She looked me in the eyes. "What?!" I said curtly. She jumped up beside me, sat down against my body and got comfy again.

Wow! I thought, that's how to do it? It's that easy? I don't have to drag around with me shackles and shadows of blaming and bitterness? I don't have to not-fully love you? And not-fully love me?

No matter what anyone unjustly blames me for, or says about me, or how they treat me, Tammy just showed me that what others do is an expression of who *they* are at the moment, not who *I* am.

Like Tammy, I can just choose to let it go!

Like Tammy, I can just choose to love, and to live a relaxed, happy life. Wow! Just letting it go! That's how to do it! I can do it!

~o~

The Social Life Of Clouds

Calca, Sacred Valley of the Andes Mountains, Peru
They come down into the valley silently, unnoticed, just before first light of dawn, in little groups of little clouds.

One by one they decide on a mountainside they like, and glide slowly toward that space.

By the time daylight comes, most of the nooks and crannies of the mountainside are occupied by a small, thin, very white cloud that's just a few feet tall. The little clouds cling to their spots for a few hours, watching the day begin, just hanging out with their friends. Next time you look, they have vanished.

Juneau, Alaska
They come in quickly, quietly, just after dawn, thick, round clouds in a great gobbling mass, sliding

down the hill on the main street.

One chooses the faded yellow building, another the wide white building, others interesting places on the hillside. Each breaks off from the mass, and moves gently toward today's object of affection. They clamp onto the buildings or the hillside, in some places blocking out little windows.

They cling to their places, watching the tourists windowshop, waiting for sun.

Summit of Mt. Washington, New Hampshire

They hit the swirling air running just before sunrise, whitish pink, whitish purple and whitish orange, waves and streams of them, elbowing each other for space.

These are not fat or fluffy or even thin clouds. These astonishing beings are slim and smooth, flowing like rivers of color in the wild wind around the top of the mountain.

As they rise and roll in the gusts, one turns toward the summit, heading straight for a woman who's standing there excited, bewitched, watching all this strange beauty.   Suddenly the woman calls out, "I've got cloud in my mouth!"

The waves and streams roll on, elbowing each other, changing colors, changing shapes, alive in the winds.

Northern Arizona

They form almost instantly, magically, pulling invisible whiteness out of the air from all directions, becoming fat-bellied, burly and thick-necked.

They tromp in their spaces in the air, and stare each other down. Then they push nearby clouds from the side, winning more space for minutes, until they too are shoved aside. Warriors, intense in territoriality.

Seattle, Washington

They run to each other, their arms outstretched,

becoming bunches of kindergarten playmates.

Hugging in huge groups they slide into small gangs and large mobs, some merry, some weeping, some just hanging around.

They chatter in teams. The littlest ones lock hands. Bigger ones lock arms. And they all dance slowly in tableaus, playing jumping and running games. Together they hold the Earth in a soft embrace.

~o~

The Mirror Me - 1

My first Spiritual Teacher gave me an exercise to do every day.

The purpose of the exercise was to practice, out loud, expressing love for myself. Learning how loving myself feels. Learning how a healthy self-esteem feels. And, over time, developing deeper feelings of appreciation for myself and deeper self-love.

I was to stand in front of a mirror and look into my eyes.

Be still.

Say out loud to my eyes, "I love you, me."

Then see what comes up in my awareness.

That face in the mirror knows everything about me, doesn't it? Even the things I don't want to face.

My Teacher said that usually what immediately comes up for people is something they *don't* love about themselves. Being overweight. Not being as kind as they want to be. Impatience. Large feet.

Being "too" young or old or tall or short. Not being athletic or mathematical or whimsical. And so on.

Hmmm...

I love you, me.

Yeah, well I *don't* love how I procrastinate, especially putting off doing things I don't want to do but should do. My mother would say... Never mind.

I love me in spite of putting things off.

I love me *including* putting things off. The reasons I give myself for putting things off are kind of cute.

Me is hugely more interesting and wonderful than doing every boring, unimportant thing on time.

I love me!

I really have beautiful eyes! I love you, me. I love seeing me smile at myself.

I like doing this. This is fun! I love you, me!

~o~

Mythticism

There's a magical land in Seattle, Washington, the city's large zoo which is actually a beautiful, lush forest hiding habitats.

Bears live there, and meerkats, and penguins and lions. I am scared of the hippopotamuses , oh all right, hippopotami, and I won't go anywhere near them.

One of my favorite places is where we can step into a myth and believe that it's real.

On the African savanna there are Giraffes. Some people can see them and some people can't.

These lovely beings are, as we know, figments of mass human hallucination, as no such animal could possibly exist on Earth. Ears like elves, sweet doe eyes, black tongues more than a foot and a half long, necks as tall as trees, velvet bodies wearing jigsaw puzzle pieces. These beings are as improbable as octopi and albatri. Oh all right, albatrosses.

Giraffes are so magical that they don't even walk! If they were actual animals we might say they lope, but they don't even lope! They glide, as though they are always ice skating.

Doing all that gliding , with their heads so far up in the sky, do they get dizzy?

And Giraffes never speak! They are speakless. How do they say "Please" and "Thank you" to each other? If they sneeze, does anyone know? When they lie down and go to sleep, do they dream in dialogue?

Silent, gliding myths. Where do they come from? And when we're not looking, where do they go?

~o~

Dancing And The Ladybugs

Every Spring, a few ladybugs would find their way from the sunny deck into my living room. What an adorable blessing!

The four cats who shared their lives with me thought the ladybugs were interesting but something of a cosmic mystery.

As pedigreed cats from centuries of being pampered and worshipped in temples, they had no concept of "prey". One cat at a time would intently watch a ladybug work hard to navigate the thick turquoise carpeting.

Clearlight Dancing was my ADHD cat and fearless athlete. He was perpetual motion when awake, and thought that the greatest fun in life was playing fetch, repeatedly chasing a wadded-up piece of paper and retrieving it to me in his teeth. But even he could never resist the lure of the slowly-moving tiny brown stowaway in our home.

Dancing was always mesmerized by a new Spring

ladybug. He would sit on the floor near her, stare and stare at her, stand up, stretch, and walk beside her for an inch or two, then sit and stare some more. Was he asking her important questions? Or was she asking him?

Always after staring and walking and staring, Dancing would eventually look up at me, slightly cross-eyed, with a worried look on his face.

And he would ask me, "Is there a *point* to all this? Is there something we're supposed to do? Or understand? Where is she going? Where did she come from? *What is this about?!"*

Ah Dancing, laddie, my dear friend. You are asking the great cosmic questions...

~o~

All Rise!

All rise.
Court is now in session.
Judge Harshly presiding.

    I figure I have two basic choices in life for how to treat myself and therefore others.

    One is that I can beat myself up, and therefore beat others up in my mind, a little bit or a lot every time I or they get something wrong, or fail, or don't notice, don't remember, don't understand, don't know how, or someone is rude to me or criticizes me.

    I can choose to be a critic. I can be right! I can choose to feel superior, angry, resentful. That way, I can be certain to keep providing my body and my emotions with a steady supply of toxic chemicals that my brain will generate because of my toxic thoughts.

Just thinking about this my belly gets tighter. I feel smaller, as though I take up less space in the air. I feel enclosed, fenced in. Not nourished.

And I can go to bed at night and lie awake wondering why life often seems hard, or boring. I can wonder why I'm not having a lot of fun, and I don't laugh much anymore. I can wonder why the last time I remember being really happy, really joyous, was when I was so much younger.

And I can be sick, my body can deteriorate, and I can wonder what life was supposed to be about.

Or, if I choose Door #2, I can congratulate myself, preferably a lot, every time I get something right, I do something well, I notice the interesting and lovely details of life, remember, understand, know how to do things, learn how to do more things, think about why I feel what I feel, make choices that I feel happy about. I can say to myself "Well done!" and smile, and feel love for me.

Instead of insisting on being right, I can insist on being happy. I can be kind, to myself and ohers. I can choose to see myself and others in a softer light, a gentler light, realizing we're all doing the best we can in any moment.

I can choose to be more compassionate and caring, praise myself and others for even little things we do and say, and I can thank people out loud when they are kind and compassionate with me.

Just thinking about all this my body feels lighter and looser, and my belly feels relaxed. I feel as though, somehow, I weigh a bit less but I'm larger, more powerful, sort of expanding in the air. I feel a quiet sense of happiness. Is this what they call "contentment"? I feel freer, as though maybe with the right wings I might be able to fly.

And I can go to bed at night smiling to myself in the darkness, thinking about how good I feel to be alive and how glad I am to be me. I can smile at how grateful I feel for so many good things that seem to cross my path and fall into my lap. I can experience how much fun it is to feel that life actually can be smooth and simple to live.

I can love how endlessly fascinating it is to constantly examine my thoughts and feelings and reactions, secretly unfolding the inner me like opening the petals of a beautiful flower, and so build an internal foundation that keeps getting stronger, that I love. What fun it is to find how much more I have to enjoy in myself and to offer to others.

And I can be merry, my body can keep getting healthier and stronger and younger, and I can see clearly that life is about choosing what I feel joyous about.

So I figure that instead of criticizing and feeling unhappy and fenced-in, I can smile in love for me and others, and feel relaxed and able to fly.

All laugh!
Playground is now in session.
Everyone rise in vibrational frequency!

~O~

Bliss By Dogsled

Across the river that rims Juneau, Alaska and into the lush and fragrant Tongass Rain Forest I rode in a van along what felt like an ancient bear path.

The little group I was in was going to enjoy the summer version of a dogsled ride.

Many mushers use a kind of all-terrain wheeled vehicle so the dogs can pull every day all year and stay healthy and happy. These vehicles seat about ten people, take fourteen dogs to pull, and everyone goes for a jaunt through the forest for a quarter of an hour or so.

No one prepared us for the surprise.

When we all piled out of the two vans at the end of the ancient bear path, the whole world changed.

A few minutes' walk from us 28 Iditarod veterans and hopefuls were hitched and waiting to pull. And when they saw us, the air turned from silent to wildly boisterous.

Dogs began jumping and yelling, dancing and singing! Woofs and arfs and yips and yipes filled the air. The dogs were giddy with sudden happiness knowing they were about to pull, and pulling is what they were born to do. "I run! I pull! I run! I pull!"

Their bliss filled the air, filled the breaths I breathed, filled my body, and I began laughing and laughing! I was filled with the joy of their happiness. I couldn't stop laughing any more than they could stop leaping.

The dogs and I in different languages shouted our delight to the trees and the ground and each other, all of us laughing and laughing!

Delirious together. Being here now together. Joy is the purpose of life, together.

When the people were seated safely in the two vehicles, the mushers told the lead dogs to run.

Instantly all was quiet as the dogs began to run. Then there were only the light sounds of tires turning on a smooth forest path and paws running on a smooth forest path.

The dogs were living their dream, being the fullness of their Song, running their dream, pulling their Song. Simple. Doing. Being. Purpose fulfilling. Love living.

As I tell this story now, my body remembers itself exhilirating down into the bones, down into every cell. The moment stays and I'm laughing now, filling with love of being.

Deliriously. Being here now-ly. Joy is the purpose of life yip yipe!

~o~

Tree At The Window

In my previous home, right outside the big south-facing bedroom lived a Douglas Fir tree. When I bought that home, the tree was a healthy and beautiful adolescent, and my four cats and I watched her grow taller and fuller year after year.

In winter in the Seattle, Washington area there isn't much snow, but if we've all lived virtuous lives during the year we might be rewarded with one or two snowfalls.

Ms. Douglas Fir loved when the snow came! My cats would sit at the window, all lined up one, two, three, four. They watched in awe as the air turned into dancing bits of white, and Ms. Fir slowly put on her new winter outfit.

Hour by hour her costume changed until, if you hadn't been paying attention during the afternoon, there she was looking like a brand new tree.

She was draped in layers of pure white, like an

old-fashioned little girl wearing layers of white petticoats.

We lived on a little hill, just high enough to bring a slight wind to us in the winter. In her snowclothes, Ms. Fir would begin to sway slightly, and wave, and then waltz in her new loveliness, showing off, prancing a bit,, shrugging her shoulders to the crowd.

What a celebration! Move, sway, bend, glide. Ms. Fir danced. She fluffed her skirts. She waved her arms. She welcomed the birds and the squirrels. She basked in her beauty and smiled to the admiring crowd. Today she was queen of the world!

~o~

The Law of Attraction

"Universe," I said out loud, "I'm not going to tell You that I need money. That would only leave me feeling that I need money, and what I'm feeling is always what I attract to me, what I cause more of to come to me. So if I felt that I need money, I would just attract more needing of money.

"No, what I'm going to say to You, Universe, is that I love love love the Reiki healing treatments I'm receiving, and the courses I'm studying, and the workshops I'm participating in, and the certifications I'm achieving, and the new people I'm meeting and the friends I'm enjoying.

"I love all this wonderment You keep sending to me in my life. It's all so fascinating and fun and enlightening. THANK YOU so much for all this expansion of me! I love my life. Every new thing I've thought of that I want to do, You have sent to me. I am so grateful!

"And I want to do more!

"So, Universe, please continue to provide me with all the resources I need to align myself with my highest divine path and purpose. Please provide me with the resources I need to be fully me, when I need them.

"I know that You know so much better than I do exactly *what* they will be and *when* I should have them. That's called Divine Timing, isn't it? So I'll leave all that how-to-do-it up to You, because You're fabulous at it.

"Is that a fully positive request, Universe? Yes, it is, because I feel happy about being me and living my life. So when I love me and love my life, what I am attracting to me is more being happy about me and more being happy about living my life. Well done, me!

"And by the way, Universe, while we're chatting, someday I would love to live in a place that I like much more than the apartment I'm living in right now. This is okay, but I don't feel that I belong in this space. I mean, it's not really *me*, y'know? There's somewhere else that's much more me. I'm thriving here, yes, and, not but, I'd like to thrive more thrivingly, when that's in divine timing, of course. Okay? So be it. Thank You thank You!"

Several weeks after this effusive monologue, the manager of my apartment building phoned me.

"I don't know if you'd be interested in this," he said, "but I have an idea and I thought I'd tell you and see how you feel about it."

He's Sun in Scorpio so he's a master at slowly, carefully sauntering and moseying toward the point.

"There's an apartment that will become available at the end of next week. The size is similar to the one you're in, but the layout is the exact opposite."

In my mind, I cringed at the thought of all the packing and moving and unpacking, and the strained muscles, and then not being able to find things for months. I wasn't super-happy where I was living, but did I really want to go through all that effort just to move to something very much the same?

"Oh," said Sun in Scorpio. "There's one last thing you might want to consider. I don't know if this would matter to you." Saunter and mosey, mosey and saunter.

"The rent on the apartment that's coming available would be $237 per month lower than what you're paying now."

Holy cow!! "YES!" I shouted into the phone.

"Universe, You're the best! I love my new place. Its energy embraces me and nourishes me every day. It feels right to me. And more money every month gives me more options in my life and I feel more free. I keep grinning! Thank You! Thank You! Thank You, Universe! You're the best!"

~o~

Comes An Ocean

He stands barefoot and barelegged in the eastern edge of the Pacific Ocean. His toes and arches and heels feel the cool, wet sand sliding slowly beneath them as the salt water pushes softly just above his ankles. The ocean says a gentle small sound as she bubbles and foams against his calves.

How long he has waited for this! How he has longed to be here!

His skin savors each caress of the ocean as his face and hair feel tiny ripples of breeze. He smiles, and his heart hums in delight.

As the ocean dances lightly around his feet, he looks beyond the blueness of the breeze past the blueness of the horizon into forever, owning forever, knowing there is nowhere to hide and everywhere to play.

The ocean's sweet deep ancient fragrance calls him back. He bends down to her little bubbles and gently touches his fingertips to the ocean's effervescence. He's surprised! It feels like being able to touch laughter. What bliss!

He loves that she is free and wild, innocent and endless, and he knows she loves that he too is free and wild, innocent and endless.

"Love of mine!" his heart calls to her, this man of lightning and magics. She comes to him, brimming with starlight and whispers. They splash into crystals of topaz and emerald and aquamarine.

He wraps himself around her, she folds herself into him, and they are home.

~o~

If I Love You

My Dad taught me how to build and tend a fireplace fire, in our 1850s Connecticut farmhouse. Sun in Virgo, he believed in getting details right and doing everything carefully and well.

Planning, choosing the right ingredients, paying continued attention, and caring. That's what makes a fire be a fire.

Scrunched sheets of newspaper with just enough air inside the scrunches to carry the tiny starter flames.

Dry, aged, skinny twigs for kindling placed on top of the newspapers, one handful for Dad but three if the firemaker was me.

Dry, aged branches and thin logs placed on top of the kindling.

Then one thick log placed at the very back against the big granite back wall of the fireplace so that it will gather and hold the heat which it will radiate to all the other logs.

These are the flame foundation, all mindfully placed with enough spacing to let the tongues of flame rise and let the fire breathe, as well as enough closeness to let the logs warm each other, keep the filames intact and encourage their eagerness to burn.

The big logs which will burn all night are placed on the fire later, when the fire is burning spread out a bit for fullest heat, when the fire knows how it wants to become.

The intention to do all of this well and with love for the fire, plus frequent and careful attention to what's happening, will show what needs to be repositioned or added or kept just as it is, always maintaining an ideal balance of closeness and space.

Space and closeness, the secrets to a successful fire which is happy to be burning, is purposeful, comforting and beautiful.

Finally, it's a wonderful help for the fire always to keep a bed of ashes underneath. If a random branch or thin log burns all the way through at its center, the two ends will have a safe, soft, contained place to fall.

This creation of joy hums, bursts into laughter, and hums again, and laughs again. It burns deeply, intensely, predictably, for as long as it is tended with loving intention and attention, giving the firemaker continual warmth, comfort and delight, embracing the firemaker in sweet earthy fragrance.

~O~

I Am All Around You

I was falled.

I didn't fall. It was a staged event. It was staged by the Universe and I was made to fall, even though there was no physical reason for me to fall.

The Universe created an event so that I could clearly see Its presence with me. And I was given the chance to learn a bit about how It communicates.

Most of all, It gave me a dramatic opportunity to choose how to feel about myself and my life, how to meet surprises, how to evaluate sudden strangers. An opportunity to change definitions and expectations that no longer served me, and to grin a lot at Its goofy sense of humor.

Walking from the grocery store, two blocks from home I crossed a very familiar street. Just as I got to the opposite curb my right ankle gave way, my right foot turned under me, and I began to fall onto the sidewalk.

I was falled.

My ankles are solid. An entire childhood of ballet, toe, tap, acrobatics, roller skating and ice skating developed ankles built like the Great Wall of China. Never before had an ankle turned, or slid underme.

Someone falled me.

As I began to fall on my right side, my body changed completely. It felt like a cat's body, moving like liquid, weightless and effortless. I was a cat, floating.

Time had disappeared. My cat body was moving very very slowly. The fall was taking minutes? Hours?

My cat body wasn't moving downward. The sidewalk moved so slowly up, up, up my leg, my hip, my torso, my arm. I noticed that if the sidewalk continued moving up like that, it would contact my face.

"No!" I thought, and pulled back my head with all the muscles in my neck and shoulders. When the fall completed, the sidewalk came to a stop less than a half-inch from my face. Well done!

"That was weird!" I thought. Lying on the sidewalk felt comfortable, and it seemed like a good idea to lie there for a minute or two to let my body gather itself together.

"Wait," I thought, "this is a busy intersection. If I lie here people will think I'm dead or broken."

I smiled and sat up, just as I heard a van side door slide open.

A tall, slim Nordic-looking woman, with straight shoulder-length hair that was so blonde it was almost white, jumped out of the van several feet from me.

"Are you all right?" she called. I could feel that this tall Nordic woman was in charge. A shorter slim man wearing a blue baseball cap jumped out of the van and slid the side door closed.

I smiled broadly to them. "I think I'm totally fine, thank you," I replied.

I saw that the van was pure white. I realized I hadn't heard any sound at all from it, no engine sound, no brakes.

The Nordic-looking woman calmly began asking me if my head hurt, or if anything hurt, was there someone I wanted them to contact, and could they take me to an Emergency Room.

She and the man, whom she called "Mike", seemed serious and centered. For my part, I felt happy, sitting on a sidewalk in the middle of a weekday, smiling.

The Nordic woman and the Mike man offered to help me stand up, and I realized that would be a good idea and I had forgotten I was still siting on the sidewalk! We three raised me in one motion to stand on my feet.

A third person now appeared from the pure white van, a short woman who told me very seriously that she was an EMT. She began asking me if I felt dizzy or weak in the legs, and other questions about symptoms.

I couldn't stop smiling. These lovely people had appeared from nowhere, out of the blue with no sound, riding in a white vehicle, and were clearly intending to spend part of this day caring for me, a total stranger, if I asked them to.

In my mind I heard "Watch for the moment. Watch for the moment," and I knew that meant the moment when I could touch each one and thank each one individually and full-heartedly.

As I said happily that I was fine and would just walk home, the moment came. They were all looking at me with continued earnestness. I reached out both my hands and held one of the Nordic woman's hands, then the EMT, then the Mike man.

"You are so beautiful," I said. "You are so gracious and kind, and I thank you for your help," I said to each one in turn.

Smiling, I waved good-bye and walked away, knowing they were watching me to see that I was all right.

Although I walked along the street in the direction the pure white van was facing, I never heard front doors open and close, a side door slide open and closed, an engine start up. Nor did I see a pure white van drive past me. When I looked back, there was no pure white van in that spot and no one standing on the sidewalk.

I wound up with one slightly skinned knee, the way children do, to let me know I had not imagined or dreamed the event. Later that day, and the next day and the next, not a single muscle in my body, especially in my neck and shoulders, hurt at all. Nothing.

Why was I falled?

To make me both a participant and an observer in a sudden, exciting tableau? To show me that my body is live energy, not the separate solid object I had always thought it was? To show me that the flow of life is much more fun than I had assumed? To help me experience myself as fearless?

Who were those three? Angels? Sent to show me that I am never alone, that I am loved, and that all is well?

~0~

A Flood Of Stars

When I was a child, on moonless nights on the farm my mom taught me the stars. In that lightless place we would go out to a field by the forest and look up. No telescope. No binoculars. Just our eyes, and Mom's delight in giving and my delight in receiving a different world.

The North Star was first, the easiest star to identify. Mom said that if I know where the North Star is I can always find my way home.

Next was Orion's belt, three almost-horizontal stars that are also very easy to spot. The constellation Orion is the home of Osiris, the ancient Egyptian god, and Mom was also teaching me Egyptology.

After that were the Big Dipper and the Little Dipper, which are really cool because they look exactly like their names.

Then came something much more complicated.

The Pleiades, a cluster of seven stars who live together in glistening beauty and brightness. Magical! I fell in love with them. The Pleiades are the home of the gods who came to Earth and began the Mayan people and the Anasazi who were the ancient ancestors of the Hopi and the Pueblo. Mom, who had walked through Chichen Itza in the Yucatan when she was still single, would later teach me about the Maya and ancient Mexico.

Thanks to my teacher, I grew up feeling like friends with the stars. A long time later I took her with me in my heart on the star adventure of my life.

Up north on the continent, into British Colombia, Canada, north of the big city of Vancouver, past any really populated places, across the lake on a ferry, I drove a friend and me to visit her parents in their home in the Canadian Rocky Mountains.

Her parents graciously invited us to dinner at a nearby small-town restaurant. They drove in the lead with my friend in their little sports car. I followed in my big black van.

It was still winter and by dinnertime the world was very dark, with no street lights, of course, just the headlights of our two vehicles.

They knew the way, and drove quickly. Within a few minutes I felt I would careen into whatever was on the side of the road if I kept driving that quickly in the darkness. They were already out of sight, around bends in the road I did not yet know were there.

I gave up. I saw what looked in the darkness like an open field beside the road and pulled over, hoping that bears and wolves might not sit relaxing in open fields at night. I knew the folks would come back looking for me.

I turned off the headlights, shut off the engine, jumped out of the van, closed the door, and stood.

Silence.

Where am I?

All around me are bits of light. Everywhere in my vision, little gold and silver lights.

Should I breathe? If I breathe, will I inhale trails

of light? Would they be fragrant?

Are they floating in the dark, like tiny fireflies? Are they pinpricks in the sky, showing me glimpses of cosmic brightness behind the dark?

More stars than sky! I hear my voice asking "Are you all the stars in the Universe come to greet me?"

Tears in my eyes, I feel a sweetness slowly swirl around me, a kinship, an urge to turn and twirl and dance with these brilliant beings, to sing with them, laugh with them.

I raise my arms to them, and my arms become streams of colors flowing upward into the lights.

We touch hands, and smiles, and souls.

Slowly I draw back my arms. I look at my hands, but in the Earth-darkness I can barely see them. There's only a faint glistening, a slight silver shimmer, just below the surface of my skin, as I begin to hear a distant sports car coming back, looking for me.

~o~

I Will Help You

Lyralen had the highest IQ of any cat I've ever known. Her job in the family was to play clever, well-thought-out practical jokes on the rest of us. And the other three cats and I laughed and loved her.

A tiny athlete with little hands, Lyralen started life as cautious, even wary, always expecting to be trampled and outdone. So to send the energy and imagery of courage and triumph to her every time I spoke to her, I named her Lyralen Rides The Stars.

It worked. It took some years but eventually she who had been terrified of motors would do a flying leap over the noisy vacuum cleaner in sheer defiance and mastery. After such feats of bravery she would reward herself by listening with me to Judy Collins music or watching her beloved NBA basketball games on TV.

She and I adored each other, and we helped

each other learn how to be love, how to give love, how to receive love.

I always wanted to pick her up and hold her, but she hated that. So I learned to expand the way I loved, to do things someone else's way, to love her the way *she* wanted to be loved, and she gave me her devotion and trust, and we loved.

Something was happening. Lyralen was losing weight, and since she had never weighed much more than a bag of feathers, I put her into her carrying case to go to her doctor.

The oddest thing began. First one cat came alone to the door grating of the closed case, and he and Lyralen looked at each other quietly for many seconds, and he walked on. Immediately, a second cat did the same. And then the third. Odd. As though they were saying a private good-bye. "Well, they know she's sick," I told myself.

Medical tests. Lyralen stayed overnight at the cat hospital. Early the next evening her doctor phoned me. Terminal. Invasive treatment might, or might not, prolong her life by a few months and might, or might not, leave her in pain. My mind blanked. I told the doctor I would phone back in the morning.

I hung up the phone, and wailed. "No! Not yet! No no no it's too soon for her to leave! Don't make me have to make this choice!"

I could hardly see through my tears. What? How?

As though my feet had their own consciousness, they walked me to a table on which some of my crystals and stones lived. My hand reached out and lifted up a strong, heavy block of Mookaite. I knew that the energy of Mookaite is very grounding and very protective. I didn't know then that Mookaite helps its person to make decisions.

I held the Mookaite against my heart because I felt that I should. I walked to the den where the other cats were, and turned on the TV to block out the truth I could not face.

For an hour I sort of watched TV, with the Mookaite sitting on my Heart Chakra. One of the cats curled up at my side. The show was distracting.

I stopped crying.

After an hour holding the Mookaite to my heart, I stood up, feeling surprisingly calm, centered, gently quiet, knowing I had chosen the way that would be easier for Lyralen. Not for me, for her. Because love, I realized, if it is anything, is joy in the other's joy of self.

Before her pain began, I could choose to help her continue riding the stars in triumph and mastery, just differently, on her way to her next lifetime.

I spoke my gratitude to the Mookaite who had removed my chaos and had calmed me down, and so had helped me to be my integrity and love.

After she moved on out of the physical, I would often see Lyralen from the corner of my eye racing down the hallway, running with one or another cat as they had loved to do.

Sometimes I can see Lyralen up there, riding the stars with star-butterflies and laughing, no doubt playing practical jokes on star-bunnies and small star-dogs.

Mookaite lives with me still. Her loving spirit sweetens the energy in my home, and her powerfulness contributes to my own strength. She calmly, patiently helps me be authentic. My friend.

~o~

Breathe

It takes me just a moment. Just a moment, to change everything. To turn worry into wonder. To flip anger to "Okay, whatever, this is my life and I can handle things". Just a moment, to replace fear with curiosity.

Breathe. Then breathe again. And then breathe once more. Ahhhh. .. Oxygen fills my bloodstream, my muscles, my organs, my cells -- changing toxins to nourishment. Isn't that weird, that air can do that? That just stopping and breathing can repair me? Just breathing in Life, breathing in Light, breathes in a higher me, my Higher Self...

Can I stop, just for a moment, and breathe in a different way of seeing? Could I breathe in the ability to see through the eyes of Source? Why not? All I have to do is ask for help. I can just request of my Guides and Angels, "Hi. Please help me learn to breathe into me a higher way of seeing, a way of knowing through the mind of Source, so that I can be more understanding and compassionate and wise." Yes! I can do that!

Breathe. Rise.

Breathe, Expand.

Breathe. Nourish myself. Ahhhh...

~o~

Changing The Past

In a gentle voice my Energy Medicine Healer told me what I had felt helpless about all my life. "You believe love is hurtful, love is pain, you don't deserve love." Despairing and true, from my childhood of continued rejection and brutality.

"You have to rewrite your story. Not to ignore what happened, but to allow you to reprogram yourself, uplift your way of thinking of yourself, and to allow a healthier version of love to manifest in your life now," my Healer told me.

Reprogram me?

I was learning that how my body and beliefs are now is mostly a result of the story of me, the picture of me, that I keep telling myself. So if my life, my reactions, my feelings and expectations are not the joyous way I want them to be, I'll have to reprogram me.

If I want happier results I need to change the beginnings.

Oh. It's that simple, huh?

Waitaminute, I get it! The old story of me that I've dragged around with me makes me feel sad and angry and smaller. So I continue to attract to me what I feel: sadness and anger and hiding.

So if I want to manifest joy, love, delight, laughter, play, abundance of all kinds, I need to change the beginnings, the programming, to joy, love, abundance and laughter.

How?

See differently.

See my story the way I *want* it to have been.

Minimize or change the things that hurt me then, and I will change how I feel now, deep down where all my definitions live.

I sat down and wrote the story of my life, reducing the horrors from pages to one sentence. The rest of the story was the good stuff of my childhood, my discovering, achieving, abundance, abilities, delights, courage, imagination, lovingness, and the other good things I was and was given.

It took three full evenings. And at the end I really felt kinder and more understanding about the people who had hurt me. I felt so much less pain. Almost no pain, actually. I didn't feel that I had to be on guard and defend myself. Relaxation seemed to spread through my muscles and mind.

A couple of weeks later I felt graciously forgiving toward the people who had hurt me. I decided to do that, to forgive them. Alone and out loud I said "I forgive you, for everything, for all time, forever." I actually felt that I weighed less!

What a surprise! I changed my story about me, and so I changed the way I feel when I tell the story or think about it. I changed the way I see myself! Gradually I let go of the burdens, the anger, the sadness that I had carried in my heart all my life. I no longer am willing to have fear and sorrow as my companions. I want a new identity!

That's the secret, isn't it! The way I feel about me is the secret to my happiness.

Two years later a different Spiritual Mentor led a group in a guided meditation. The Teacher suggested inviting someone into our meditation, someone whom we wanted to forgive.

Magic! Instantly, my imagination brought in the two people who had been so negative in my old story of me.

I imagined the three of us in our living room when I was a child, one standing on my left, one on my right. And I changed everything.

Quite the opposite of what used to happen, I imagined them smiling to me, looking with happiness at me, talking to me, asking me about me with smiles and genuine interest in me. When I answered in my imagination, they were happy to hear what I had to say.

First one, then the other, hugged me and held me tightly, kissed my cheek, carressed my face, and looked me in my eyes with love radiating from them to me. As they held my hands, we all laughed happily together, loving and being loved. I felt that I was someplace where I belonged.

I let myself enjoy this experience for some minutes, to allow the love and the sweetness to become part of my memory, part of me.

Then in my imagination I put the three of us at

our country home, in the back yard past the woodpile, near the well, doing a chore together. Again, I placed them standing on either side of me, smiling, happy. They touched my arms, held my hands, laughed in love, hugged me, and looked into my eyes with delight at being with me.

When I came out of the meditation, I wept. I had just lived the childhood I had always wanted, one in which I was loved and paid attention to and made to feel important by people whom I could love and enjoy and trust.

Miraculous and simple! I created in my mind a visualization using imagined sight, sound, touch and emotion. I created new programming for me, a new story of me. A vivid story I saw and heard and felt joyfully in my heart.

The story with hugging and happiness is the story I now carry with me. It's the story I now live.

I changed my past and the way I feel about me. Changing my past changed my present, and my future.

~o~

Say Thank You To The Nice Lady

Going home from the office I stepped off the
bus, crossed the street, and noticed in the corner of
my eye something moving.

A mother Mallard Duck and a burble of very tiny,
brand new baby ducks bobbing beside her.

Delighted at the sweet sight, I stopped for a
moment to watch them coming down slowly from
the top of a little grassy hill, toward the sidewalk --

and directly in line to walk right into a four-foot-
deep open hole in the ground. It must have been
left uncovered from water or electricity work.

Panic ran through my body!

Mom Mallard was murmuring a gentle word or
two every few seconds and the babies were chirping
and cheeping and having a wonderful First Field Trip.

What to do? No other human was in sight to
help. How could I save them and not frighten
them?

Without thinking I began to stretch my arms way

out on either side of my body, and I crouched just a little, feeling like a condor. Walking slowly toward them, I began chanting in a normal speaking volume but a low, authoritative pitch.

"Go back. Go back. Go back. Go back."

Mother Mallard said one word. In an instant, the mother and seven tiny babies all turned as one, back the exact way they had come.

Slowly followed by a chanting human condor, the family topped the hill, turned a corner toward tall bushes and what I knew was their home at a little lake, and walked out of sight.

I felt slightly insane about having suddenly become a condor for a few minutes. And I also felt a little giddy as an instrument of the Universe sent on that day at that moment to save the ducks.

As the babies' chirps faded into the distance, I waited a bit to be sure Mother didn't change her mind, and then I walked home with tears of gratitude and joy in my eyes.

The odds of all seven babies surviving were low. I knew that every year baby ducks and baby geese disappeared from that lake during the nights, to neighborhood owls and kestrels and cats. Well, I thought, at least they had fun and adventure today on their First Field Trip.

Two months passed before I had a chance to visit the little man-made lake where the ducks lived. I wanted to see who was there that day.

I walked a path all around the small lake, seeing no ducks or geese., so I decided to go home.

Over a tiny hill about thirty feet away came a female Mallard duck surrounded by a group of almost-grown ducks.

I stood perfectly still. The female stopped walking and looked at me.

Softly she said one word. The entire group of almost-growns instantly turned and began walking calmly toward me.

Seven! There were seven! I knew who that mother Mallard was.

The gang gently gathered around my feet, saying soft little sounds, pecking at bits on the path and bits at the edges of my shoes. Seven! They all survived!

I turned my head toward their mother thirty feet

away, who was looking at me. I sent her a silent thank-you-thank-you-thank-you with my gratitude and love. I could feel her receiving my message and feeling my love! She turned her head and looked off into the distance. She knew her children were safe with me!

I didn't move a muscle as the gang milled about my feet, very close to my body. Such sweetness! Such intimate trust! All I could do was grin.

One word Mom spoke softly. The children calmly turned away from me, still murmuring to each other, and slowly ambled back to the top of the tiny hill. When they joined Mom again, all of them walked toward the lake and out of sight.

I stood transfixed. She knew me! She remembered me! She sent her children to me. I wondered if the Universe told her somehow that maybe I saved the lives of her babies.

If I never do another good thing in my life, I have done this, and my life has mattered. If I ever needed to be shown that we are all in this together, I have been shown.

~O~

Dreamtime In The Hills

The beginning was creation, when life began, called "Dreamtime" in the deeply mystical Australian Aboriginal culture.

At the beginning of all is innocence...

I give you my body as I have never given to any lover.
I give you my life as I have never given to anything.
I face you clearly, eagerly, joyously, knowing I must think and feel and believe my way around you. I can't wait I can't wait!
I face you knowing I have lived all my life to be with you, to experience me with you and through you, to share our being different beings. I can't wait I can't wait!
And I know that when I face you, you are facing

me, learning me, understanding me, agreeing to accept me, as I am learning you, understanding you, agreeing to trust you, planning to trust myself.

I stand before you, offering to you and to me the very finest of which I am capable. You stand before me offering to me the pure, the naked integrity of your life, and offering to teach me your secrets which you hide from most others, and which will help me teach myself my most secret, pure, naked integrity. Oh man I can't wait!

We begin.

I choose a fingerhold, and another, and a toehold, and another. You signal your approval by holding me. I reach higher and wider for a new fingerhold, and for another, raising my feet, raising my body. You approve, and you hold me.

As I choose, and rise, I know you in my toes, my ankles, my calves my knees my thighs. Your granular skin rasps against my clothes, responding to me as I press my body to you, my chest shoulders arms hands fingers, my fingerprints. I know each moment of you in my skin and flesh, my muscles and nerve endings.

You bring me in, knowing that to stay alive I must press closer to you, be as much of you as becoming you. You hold me. I hold you. You hold me.

Slowly you give me your secrets. Quickly I give you the secret best that I am. I know you will never tell my secrets. You know I will never tell yours. Who is pressing to whom? Who is revealing self?

As I climb your secrets, in this moment that has never been before are we creating a new me? As you hold me in my rising, in this moment which is new for both of us are we creating a new you?

I step, and suddenly slip, my foot ssliding. *Vulnerable!* I grasp you I grip you you hold me *fear!* I stop, and let that wave flow through me, and out of me. I breathe, breathe, breathe, alive. Clinging like this I feel ungraceful, and grateful. Who is clinging to whom?

I step in a new toehold, watching my courage unfurl in me again, feeling my love for me flower in me.

Reaching the top, I plant my feet firmly on you and, raising my arms to the sky, I laugh and laugh! I take a deep breath and shout a long, long, loud yell I am king I am great I am all things fabulous and strong and glorious I am! I belong being in my life! I belong being me! This hard work, this hard play, is part of my Divine Work, the divine emergence of my shining magnificence. I belong being me!

When the light is leaving the sky and I am driving back home to the city, I marvel at how much music begins in me when I am with you, how much openness and trust and sweet exhilaration *about me* keep growing in me, as I do so well something so difficult as being completely in tune with you, completely in tune with myself, resonating in harmony and vibrating in the rhythms of your life and mine all at once.

I will remember being with you, the feel of you, the smell of you, the small scraping sounds of you, the way your body resisted me and welcomed me. And I will wonder if you still feel my shoes in your toeholds, my smooth pants against your scratchy skin, my shirt stretching across you, my fingertips pressing into you.

I love the cleverness I am when I am with you. I love the excellence I am becoming because of you. And the becoming just keeps on becoming, doesn't it?

I love who I am! I am bravely and brillianttly being the Who I Am, experiencing My Creation, being My everything I can invent to be in the moment.

I am the fulfillment of my dreams! I am the creator, and the creation, of my new dreams! I am being me, and so I am being Me.

At the beginning of all are innocence, and freedom.

In the unfolding of all are laughter, and love.

~O~

My Porpoise

The legend of the sacred Crystal Skulls says that twelve skulls of perfect quartz crystal, about the size of an adult human head, were gifted to humanity in the time before time and placed in different locations around Earth.

Quartz is a wonderful and powerful worker. It absorbs information and energy, records and stores it, broadcasts it, and emits its own clear and uplifting energy frequency.

The benefactors, the ones who gave humanity the Crystal Skulls, were our ancestors from the stars and the heavens, with the intention to provide teachers, in the form of the sacred Crystal Skulls, to assist humanity in its path of evolving enlightenment.

Each Skull is said to radiate very strong energies of teaching and of help and support to humanity. Each Skull specializes in a field, such as scientific excellence, spiritual and physical healing, or recording in real time the history of the planet. Each becomes active when the time comes for it to be discovered and go to work.

The Mitchell-Hedges Crystal Skull specializes in healing, and emanates both healing energy and healing teaching to humans who are in his presence.

One summer day I had the extraordinary opportunity to be near the Mitchell-Hedges Crystal Skull for close to five hours. From the moment I heard about his visit I knew completely and happily that I must be with him, that his visit was part of my path.

In a lecture hall with scores of other people, I sat in the front row just a few feet from the Crystal Skull who sat on a small table facing the audience.

After the talk given by the current steward of the Skull, each participant was able to approach the Crystal Skull and place their hands not on him but in his aura around him, less than a foot away from him.

In addition, I simply placed myself near the Crystal Skull for long periods of time. I didn't feel like a groupie. I just felt I was doing what I was supposed to do, doing my work, bringing into me whatever energies he would radiate to me.

Later in the afternoon, in a much smaller room the Mitchell-Hedges Crystal Skull received private visitors, by ones and twos, for fifteen-minute Skull-to-human connecting.

A man I didn't know had graciously agreed a week previously to share his session with me. When directed, he and I entered the little room.

In the soft lighting, the Crystal Skull sat on a black cloth covering an ordinary card table. The man who was the steward of the Skull was sitting on the other side of the table, the other side of the Crystal Skull. We all said quiet hellos, and the man I didn't know and I sat in card-table chairs in front of the Crystal Skull.

The steward urged us to bend in a bit and look at the cranial area of the Crystal Skull. "A shape just appeared," he said, "as you were walking into the room. Do you see the porpoise?" he asked.

"Now and then," he told us, "a shape will appear

spontaneously in the top area of the head of the
Crystal Skull. I don't know how it happens. I just
know it happens. In the more than two decades I've
worked with the Skull, I've never seen the shape of a
porpoise before. Isn't that interesting? Here, I'll
turn the Skull a bit. Do you see the porpoise more
clearly?"

He said the word "porpoise" three times. I knew
that the number three represents manifestation of
the divine in the physical. So I immediately knew
that the sudden appearance of the porpoise shape
was a message, a divine message, a clear and
specific message to the person for whom the word
"porpoise" had meaning.

The man I didn't know ignored the shape and
immediately began asking the steward unrelated
quesitons. So the porpoise idea was not meant for
him.

Only one moment in my life has had anything to
do with "porpoise". Just seven minutes into my very
first session receiving intuitive Energy Medicine, my
Healer and I made a joke together about one's
divine "porpose" in life, instead of saying "purpose",

and we laughed together. The Skull's message was meant for me.

Something else important was being woven by the Universe into the fabric of this event. Over a period of more than a year, I told my Healer, a holy and merry man, several times, "I want to be in the way of being that you are," in other words holy, merry and healing.

The porpoise shape that appeared inside the Mitchell-Hedges Crystal Skull was a message to me. "Here is your purpose." That my life purpose is healing. That healing is my work. That the healing energy of the Crystal Skull and the healing energy of me are in this work together.

I sat and meditated in the presence of the Crystal Skull. When the time came to leave, I and the man I didn't know thanked the steward and walked out of the room.

One of the facilitators of the Skull's visit asked us, "How was your experience?"

The man I didn't know said enthusiastically it was wonderful, adding, "I've never before felt energy like that. I'll have to think about it."

I gasped in sudden recognition. *I know that energy!* I exclaimed, "The energy of the Crystal Skull is *exactly the same* as the energy of my Healer!"

How can that be? How can something that is quartz and something that is human radiate the same energy?

The Skull and my Healer are the same energy in intention, purpose and work. Both radiate divine love and compassion. Both express the Universe's sweet and goofy sense of humor. And both live happily as instruments of divine love and healing in the world.

Wow... and the Crystal Skull was telling me what other seers had told me, the truth that I was coming to know in my heart, that I am joining him and my Healer in intention, purpose, work, love and compassion, and humor.

The facilitator had an interesting response to my exclamation. She said that in her experience over the years, she finds that the Crystal Skull radiates *to* people the energy that *they* are...

The Universe speaks to us all the time,

everywhere. This time, the Song was a sweet joke known by only two people on Earth, and then known throughout the Universe, and gently gifted back to me to show me I am loved, I am never alone, all is well, and my dreams are coming true.

~O~

Ripples

Everything is energy.

The rain comes as busy tiny silver hands, touching everything, bathing everything.

The snow comes silently scattering bits of starlight, touching everything, bathing everything.

The sunlight comes on the cymbal sound of "I am by golly I am", touching everything, bathing everything.

The moonlight comes riding on the thoughts of owls, touching everything, bathing everything.

They change everything.

Everything is energy. My feelings are energy. My beliefs are energy. My thoughts. My words. My actions. All energy.

They are me radiating from me in all directions, touching everything, bathing everything.

I change everything.

Choose my ripples with intention, with awareness and compassion, kindness and love.

~o~

Singing The Song

The morning Stars sang together,
and all the Angels shouted for joy.
- Job 38:7

High 5!

How do you suppose They react, our Spirit Guides and Angels, when we follow Their advice?

They are always working hard in our highest good, helping us and guiding us toward choices that will nourish us, choices that will make us feel deeply happy. They are sending us messages, constantly, every day, messages that seem to us like random ideas out of the blue. Our Angels and Guides hope we notice the interesting, unconnected ideas that pop into our minds, and They hope we follow Their suggestions.

When we do, do you suppose They grin in delight, and jump and shout "YAY!", and go around high-fivin' each other, splashing particles and beams of Light in all directions?

~o~

Who's Minding The Moon?

When I was a child in America I was told we can see the shape of the face of a man on the surface of the Moon. When I was an adult in Japan I was told we can see the shape of a rabbit on the surface of the Moon.

Now, of course, we have tons of scientific research photographs of the Moon.

And now we know there are structures on the surface of the Moon, which have actually been seen since the end of the 19th Century. Buildings and things. Architectural shapes. Bridges. Pyramids. Obelisks or spires, including one that's the height of a fifteen-story building.

Astronauts have seen beams of light and flashes of light coming from the Moon. And moving lights and reflected lights. And puffs of smoke.

Very ancient texts tell that the earliest humans said there was no moon in the sky when humanity began. These people told that the Ms. Moon we know was placed near Earth to assist in human development, and that she was, well, wrangled, pulled here, and placed in her current location in the very old times before ancient time began. But I think that wrangling and pulling sound like Earth ideas, not Moon ideas.

I know that, just like humans and mice and mountains, Moon agreed to do the work she contracted to do as her divine mission. So I'm pretty sure she glided into place by herself. Or maybe she had help from friends and she danced into place on the vibrations of a musical note, or even an entire song.

Where did she come from? I know that I am a spiritual being having a human experience, so I know that the Moon is a spiritual being having a moon experience. I came from a whereabouts before Earth, so I know that Moon came from somewhere. I wonder what the full truth is of her divine path and purpose.

The scientists say that there are more structures on the side of the Moon we never see than there are on the side we do see. On the mystery side are there playgrounds, and libraries, solar panels, and Saturday night dances?

Are there schools that teach integrity, spiritual perception, and the power waiting within emotional vulnerability?

Do they teach about seeing with compassion, and working with the natural flow of Universal Energy?

Do they teach about not feeling afraid but instead feeling curious?

Do they teach how to love without limit?

Do the Moon People gaze at Earth every night and wonder how we're doing? Do they hope they will come here someday?

When they come to Earth to visit us, will they use a passport? Or will they use a passportal?

~0~

Partners In Secret

In the foyer of his house, the man I had gone to visit said, a bit apologetically, "I hope you don't mind too much. My dog tends to jump up on people to welcome them." The man stood with his hand down, just lightly touching his dog's shoulder, perhaps to infuse into the dog the intention of not jumping up on me.

"No problem," I said quietly.

I looked down into this beautiful dog's intelligent, soulful, laughing eyes. The instant his muscles began to move in order to jump up on me, my wisdom from loving dog whispering shows on TV blossomed. I quietly brought my open hand between the dog and me. No words. No other movement.

This lovely dog stopped. All his muscles relaxed. He was looking up at me with comprehension and interest in his eyes. She's part of the Pack Leader, he decided.

He stood quietly in the foyer observing the conversation between the man and me.

The man casually invited me to go into the living room and make myself comfortable while he went to the kitchen to get tea.

The dog had disappeared, probably finding nothing worth his attention in the human conversation. I was now alone in the foyer.

I walked into the living room and turned toward the place on the sofa where I had sat the previous time I was there.

Standing still on that place on the sofa was the dog, happy, confident and curious, smiling directly to me.

"Okay, Ms. Pack Leader," his energy was saying to me, "what now?"

I looked in his eyes, enjoying his audacity. He radiated a comfortable ownership of the house, and at the same time he was clearly accepting me as friend game-player.

No words. No sounds. No movement. We looked in each other's eyes. He waited. The ball was in my court.

I silently pointed my finger and moved my hand, once, pointing from the sofa to the floor.

"Oh, okay," he said, and jumped to the floor. He turned around and looked up at me. "Thank you," said my energy to him. "Cool!" he answered, and as I smiled he turned and walked out of the room.

Knowing the man's personality, I was pretty certain that standing on the sofa was not a permitted behavior in that home. So I didn't tell the man that his beloved and intellectually adventurous dog had stood on the sofa.

The dog didn't tell him either.

A sweet secret. A sweet experience.

~o~

The Flying Cat

Lyralen Rides The Stars was all muscle and brains, with the highest IQ of any cat I've known packed into her little six-and-a-half-pound body. She decided that her joyous purpose in life was to play practical jokes on the rest of the family.

Lyralen and I lived with three male cats, so as the only girls we would tell each other our girl secrets and tattle on the boys.

One of Lyralen's favorite pastimes involved getting to a high surface, like the top of an antique cupboard or of a tall cat condo. Then she would wait until no one was thinking about her anymore and cats were just calmly walking around, living their lives.

Suddenly, this bundle of coiled springs would leap off the high surface, straight out into the air, head and arms stretching forward, legs and tail stretching back.

And this little being sailed, soared, flew straight

out into the room and actually stayed level for a moment or two!

A surprised cat and I would look up in amazement as, several feet out from where she had started, Lyralen began flying downward, always landing in a safe, clever place as we watched. Then she would jump to the back of the sofa or walk off toward another room, as though what she had just done were the most normal thing in the world.

Cats do not jump that way from higher places to lower ones. They look downward, their heads face downward, and their arms and legs point downward, because they are going downward. Very logical!

I often wondered why Lyralen flew straight out into the air the way she did. "Because she can," was usually my laughing answer. But I felt there was more to it than that. Why would she even think of doing such a thing? Cats don't do that! And why didn't she learn from observing the three other cats that flying is not what cats do?

One day I made a list of the many ways Lyralen did *not* do things catly. The messy way she drank water, as though she had no idea how to lap up liquid. The way she insisted on being high up to eat, sleep, wash or observe the world. The way she quickly vanished when a human walked into the room. And even the way she behaved with me, whom she adored, as though she was too small and might be trampled. How her voice was a high-pitched "EEK!", a shriek that sounded not like a cat but like a bird.

Ohmygosh! Is this the first time she's ever been a cat? Has Lyralen's soul spent many lifetimes being a bird? Of course! A parrot, perhaps the smartest bird. Yes! It all fits! She's adapting her soul-memories of how to live life to her new experience in a cat body.

I was witnessing reincarnation. I was witnessing, and helping, this glorious being transition in her soul's evolution. I am honored, Lyralen, that you chose me to trust.

Will we meet again, my baby girl, the next time you're a cat or a time after that? Of course we will, because we had so much fun and love together, and love is eternal.

~O~

This Time

This time, my friend is younger, much younger than I, forty-two years younger! She sees everything Earthly in a way I don't think of because I didn't learn it that way. And so she teaches me a million things I never would have understood if I did not love her. And I teach her wisdom and my way of seeing which is so different from hers. And neither of us objects to the differences, nor feels envious of the separate visions and wisdomes. Instead, we each look forward, as children do, to seeing a new vista, hearing new music, because of the other.

My Guides are showing me that this time we are not little together, and I don't have to hold her hand tightly as we cross the gently-running river close to our horses. I hear the splashing of our hands and feet against the water, and the splashing of the water against the bodies of our horses. We will look for food, and grass for the horses, and a place for all of us to sleep, and maybe grown-ups to help us. This time I don't have to protect and provide for her, and she does not have to worry that I too might disappear from her.

This time, as my wise and loving uncle she does not have the sole and sweet responsibility of teaching me how to be a man when I grow up. He taught me well, and in time I hoped he watching me from heaven and felt proud of the man like him that I became.

I'm seeing that this time, I don't have to care for her and hold her thinned and weakened lovely body in my shaking arms as her light slips away and I become without her. Or was it she who had to let me go, ahead of her?

This time, we live in cities, ride in cars, have phones and freezers and free deliveries to our front doors. This time, we are not getting up at dawn, hitching up our one horse, plowing the fields, planting the crops. We are not sweating, tired, knowing this is what there is to do. I bend down and pick up a full hand's worth of dark soil. I hold the good dirt to my nose, and smell the richness of its magic, this bed that births and grows our foods. I am proud to be a farmer. I am proud to feed the people. I drop the handful of soil back where it belongs, and speak to our horse, and plow some more.

This time, we are each a shining pillar of light, seeing the same way each other sees, bringing to each other our baskets full of flowers and moonlight and small furry animals. This time, we cross the meadows together, naming the stones and the trees as we go, laughing with the birds, knowing that, this time, we can be sisters walking nearby paths at last, living the dream we have dreamed together for so long, the soul family dream, the dream of helping each other to anchor the ascension of Earth. We laugh, and laugh some more, and chop wood and carry water. And it is as perfect as we have dreamed.

~0~

The I Am Presence

Riding on the narrow-gauge train from Cuzco, Peru, which I had picked up at Ollantaytambo, I was quietly thrilled that there were no more stops between here and Aguas Calientes, the town nearest Machu Picchu. Just the land and the life on it, from here to the end of the line. I settled in to watch, and enjoy.

The train was moving at a very modest pace north from the end of an agricultural valley at about nine thousand feet above sea level. For millennia, Valle Sagrado, the Sacred Valley, has been growing abundant crops for the people of Peru.

On farms, the chickens, dogs, horses, llamas and occasional alpacas looked up momentarily at the familiar moving train. Then the train reached the end of the valley.

Quickly, out the windows everything narrowed. The train's right-of-way was now just a single set of tracks. Instead of open farms, I was watching in amazement a complete change of climate.

The elevation above sea level lowered and the green growing things became dense, dark green, with thick leaves that were long and wide.

We were at the beginning of the high jungle! Moving into the "cloud forest", the train slowed down to a crawl as rugged mountains edged in, on their slide into multi-green lushness.

The craggy side of the Andes Mountains seemed to be just inches from the right side of the train, maybe only a hand's length from the windows.

In the last five minutes, my train had become a slow intruder, curling around bends in the mountainside, now moving a little right, now a little left, now finding a short space in which to move straight ahead.

What a feat of engineering!

On the left, the wild and powerful Urubamba River was jumping and dancing in its path that was still fairly narrow. The river would grow wider and deeper as it ran its long road down to become a source of the Amazon River.

And on the other side of the river, still close enough to the train to display the details, were more mountains. But these were terraced, a method of agriculture used in the Andes for thousands of years.

Narrow flat surfaces were long ago sliced into the sides of the muontains, layer after layer like steps up the mountain. Each step is only a few feet from the edge to the body of the mountain, just enough space for crops to receive sunlight and rain and for a man to tend them, and no space at all for any machinery.

Someone else tended these terrace farms. Bulls, helping the humans to turn the soil, plant the crops, weed and harvest. For centuries bulls have been the tillers of this soil, the managers of the Andean terraces. In their robust strength and gentle patience, they help to feed the people of the Andes.

In the clear morning light, I suddenly saw one of them.

Not far from the slowly-moving train and therefore easy to see, the bull was not working at the moment. He was standing still near the edge of a terrace, calmly looking down at my train. Now he seemed to be looking directly at my window, and at me. Had my attention to him drawn his attention to me?

He glowed! A bright, deep golden light radiated from the bull, shining clearly, extending three or four feet in all directions from his body.

Glowing. Golden. Completely confident, contented and peaceful, a being who knew he was respected and loved and cherished. He was the owner and giver of all his excellent work. The owner and caretaker of the mountainside. The owner and bestower of life.

The bull living his divine path and purpose offered the integrity and clarity of his being to anyone who came near. Glowing. Golden.

As my train slowly passed him, I thought he turned his head just a bit to follow my face following his face. I'm not sure if he did. But I do know he showed himself to me, in every way that matters, his inner self, his soul, one being revealing himself to another.

The beautiful bull gifted me with Grace. Glowing. Golden. Purposeful, peaceful and pure.

~o~

Spiritual Dishwashing

"Meditation? I have no time to sit, doing nothing, and meditate," I replied to someone's suggestion.

"Gratitude? I have no time to interrupt my life and just sit around every day writing a list of things I feel grateful about," I replied to someone's suggestion.

"Appreciation? What do you mean stop walking and say out loud to a flower or a tree or a squirrel that I think they're marvelous? I have no time for such frivolity," I replied to someone's suggestion.

In the weeks that followed, I found myself, oddly, surprisingly, doing some things more slowly than usual.

I found myself washing more dishes by hand, telling myself that my intention was to be sure they were clean, so that I would be pleased.

The soothing sound of the running water seemed to become background music, audible enough to be part of my experience, and constant enough to forget. Adding hot or cold until my skin felt happy, I noticed how wonderfully soft the water felt, how it shaped itself to the shape of my hand, how comforting it felt.

I held the blue sponge in the stream of water, squeezed the sponge until it gurgled and made me laugh, soaked it again, and sudsed the sponge to a satisfying froth. How clean the soap smelled!

A plate with stuck bits of food. Rubadubdub with suds and sponge. Scrub. Scrub. Rubadubdub. Turn the plate to the other side. Rubadubdub. Rinse and watch trails and rivulets of water flowing down the plate, chasing soapy bubbles away away away. The plate becomes smooth and clear and bright. I have done well. I love my excellence!

A soup bowl. The chance to use my hands more cleverly, to turn the bowl with one set of fingers while sudsing and rubadubbing with my other set of fingers. Turn turn rub rub. Ah rinsing! No clear streams here. Instead, the running water that feels just right on my skin is turning and swirling, suds flowing in circles, down, away. Clean and beautiful. My thumb deliberately squeaks the surface, just for fun.

Spoons and forks and knives. The flowing water splashes lightly, leaping freely from them in all directions. Holding three or four at a time in one hand, suds'em suds'em rubadubdub. Rinsing water all mixed up in different shapes.

The water is having so much fun!

Clinkle clankle as they settle down to drain.

Squeeze the sponge. Resuds. Wash the countertop. Wash the other countertop. Wash inside the sink and all around it. Along the top of the faucet give a friendly rub from back to front. Squeeze, rinse, squeeze, rinse. Rub the suds from the counters and splash the suds from the sides of the sink. Rinse and squeeze and prop the sponge where it will dry.

Turn the water off.

Silence.

Sparkling.

I am virtuous! I do excellent work! I am who I

always wanted to be when I grew up!

I have just spent a part of my life alone with the water and my hands and the quiet of my mind.

Slipping into my excellence, I have meditated by giving my full attention to the event, beyond thought. No yesterday or last year, no tomorrow or next year. Now. Me.

Slipping into what I do well, I have felt gratitude for this experience of doing this thing well. No regrets. No comparisons. Me. Being.

Slipping into enjoying the water and the suds and my excellence, I have appreciated me and the sights and sounds and feels. Now. Me. Being.

So this is what spiritual practice is about... Paying attention. Being the experience. Enjoying being me, one daily event at a time.

Spiritual dishwashing.

Being me now.

What do I want to do next? Shop for groceries?

Oh, wait, I want to email that online seller that I haven't yet received what I ordered.

What is my intention? Peacefulness, simplicity, kindness. Okay. Slip into my excellence. Spiritual emailing. Okay.

~o~

The Faerie Who Lives On My Shoulder

I fall into fits of happy laughing. While thinking at home. Walking down the street. Listening to music. Silly, happy, merry laughter.

Especially in the past few years, I remember something goofy, or flip thughts backwards in my mind, and I'm gone! And then I don't care about anything except how good I feel!

My first Reiki Healer showed me that happy laughing raises our vibrational frequency, so I fall into this nuttiness with glee.

And I know who nudges me and tickles my perceptions and would get me sent to the Principal's office if I were an actual child.

There's a Faerie who lives on my left shoulder, often sitting there leaning back against my neck. She's a Goddess Faerie who's the Queen of her tribe, very sparkly with little golden wings, a beautiful gown, an elegant golden crown and a tiny scepter.

She's with me for all of my life as one of my Spirit Guides. In the many years when I was serious and afraid, she must have been working hard to keep me afloat.

When she's not making me laugh, she covers my face in kisses, adorable little faerie kisses.

This magical Guide is one focused and determined divine teacher, helping me every day to know how to raise my frequency by really enjoying being me and and practicing it.

My Goddess Faerie has taught me how to notice faeries, sprites, elves, and other Elementals in the backyard gardens of my friends and in the small forests that live outside office buildings and parking lots.

So I get to teach people that they have beautiful winged helpers near them, and I've found that they love knowing that, and laugh in delight.

The secrets and the gifts of the Universe show up for us in the most unexpected and the loveliest ways, don't they?

~O~

Bus Stop Tree

Such a pretty tree, so straight and strong, her branches in balanced fullness. She lived at the bus stop nearest a supermarket I rarely went to so I guess I never really looked at her before. Such a pretty tree.

I stood waiting for the bus, admiring the symmetry and robust health of the tree.

Feeling appreciation and enjoyment and love, I stepped close to her, and placed my left hand with the palm fully open on the trunk of the tree.

A rush of gratitude flowed from her into my hand, into my mind! Not just love, gratitude. A river of emotion flowed from her to me.

Tears came to my eyes in thanks to the tree for her honesty and openness, for her sweet and intimate gift. For several seconds, as I held my hand to her skin, she blessed me with the beauty of her heart, the integrity of her consciousness.

~o~

Synchronicity Salmon

In the Pacific Northwest of the U.S. we love eating Alaskan salmon. Especially when we can buy it on sale!

At my favorite fishmongering supermarket, I bought four pounds of this fabulous food, all of it cut into quarter-pound steaks, please.

On my way home, out of the blue I began thinking about someone who is a wonderful person and a really good friend. I thought, I want to give him some of this marvelous salmon since I have so much.

Well that's a surprise! Being generous is very nice and all, I thught, but I can't afford to go handing out salmon. But I have this strong feeling that I want to. But that's less for me, and didn't I go to the store for me, not anyone else? But I have the strong feeling that I want to.

At home I chose four very nice steaks, wrapped

them together, and went to find my friend to give him the salmon. He was, as usual, pretty busy working and somewhat distracted, but he was happy to receive the salmon.

The next day we ran into each other. His face lit up as he told me how happy he was about the salmon.

As it turned out, well, as the Universe knew and was urging me to pay attention to my own inclinations, he was so busy the previous day at work that the only thing he ate all day was a bagel, and when he left work to go home he was both starving and exhausted.

He told me that he was so joyful to suddenly have a whole pound of salmon, and he grilled and ate the entire pound! We laughed! I was amazed, and elated that I had given him, on the very day he needed it, something that would make his evening effortless and fun and nutritious.

They call all that "synchronicity". Good ol' Universe setting things up in the way they need to happen. It really knows how to weave wishes, possibilities, personal growth choices, and blessings all together, doesn't It? Kind of like composing a beautiful song...

A few days later my friend gave me a pound of marvelous locally-raised grass-fed ground beef from one of his rancher friends in this area.

Blessings by the pound? And sometimes we wonder if anyone out there is paying attention to us... I have to smile . "Anyone" is having a lot of fun doing all that clever weaving, making loveliness show up in the most surprising ways.

~o~

Gasping For Air

Noon in August in the heavy heat of New York City. I was a ten-year-old child walking home alone from the store. The dense humidity pressed against my lungs and the quiet heat seared my skin.

I felt a small sound.

I looked to the street, the black pavement. The ground under the street was gasping for breath.

The street heaved upward a bit, Earth underneath pushing to take in some air.

Everywhere I glanced the ground was covered. Tall, heavy buildings surrounded the street. The only places for Earth to breathe were the tiny spaces in the concrete sidewalks where lone trees were allowed to drink the rain.

Are those little spaces enough breathing room for Earth in the city? How can she get relief in this heat? Can I help her at all? Is there any life left under the pavement?

~o~

You're A Silly, Silly Mountain!

Every time I drive on highway I-90 east from Seattle, Washington I have the most wonderful experience. When I go past the town of Issaquah almost to North Bend, there's a place where the highway goes in front of a small hill. Then the road curves a bit left.

And bang! There he is, Mount Si, straight ahead staring at me. He's not pointy but round on top, and fat and round all around, and not very tall at all.

Hi, Si!

The instant I see him he starts me laughing. Is he laughing *for* me? Is he laughing *with* me? I think the latter, but it doesn't matter. He just makes me laugh and laugh and laugh. I smack the heel of my hand on the stering wheel, on the seat. I stomp my free foot on the floor.

Okay, I say. I'll pull over.

I pull over, put the car in Park, and just sit there

laughing. My cheeks hurt! My belly hurts! Even my ears hurt!

What is it with this mountain that he always makes me laugh? I know: he's radiating laughter because that's where the loggers from long ago buried the Secret Treasure of The Ancient Gigglers. That's why!

Or, or waitaminute.

When he was growing up Mt. Si watched too much TV and it stunted his growth. And now he thinks he's Monty Python. "I say, you'd best mind that dead fish wot you're 'olding in your 'and not to smack me in the face with it, eh wot?" Yeah, that's it! Python Si, loving life.

~o~

Awakening

Instead of taking a nap as I had expected, I lay in silence for an hour one afternoon, eyes closed, thinking.

Then out loud I asked the Universe, "How can I end my lifelong habit of inventing reasons to feel sorry for myself? How can I stop turning on that circular torture trail? How can I look differently at me, and at events in my life?"

Instantly she stood in the air above me, a woman of immense power, integrity, compassion, courage and beauty.

She wore a long dark robe of ancient design. I had not thought of her in that flesh-and-blood way since I was a girl.

Brünhilde, the heroine of Richard Wagner's masterpiece operas, carefully taught to me and shared with me by my mother.

Half goddess, half human, the spiritual warrior Brünhilde loved magnificently and unconditionally, lost everything, and chose to ascend from anguish to redeem the world through Divine Love.

Hers is the transcendent music I have loved always, music I've heard as a rising arc of shimmering golden light.

Seeing her now I knew *this* was the answer to my questions. The majesty and the dream of who I am. Long ago I put this all aside, when I was young, as too sacred, too big to achieve.

The Universe sent me exactly this vision to remind me of who I always believed I am. To offer me this possibility, which I myself chose long ago, to turn my self and my life into this magnificence.

Do something I know how to do, I thought, which my Spiritual Teacher taught me. Reunite that dream and me, that heroine and me. Bring her and her destiny back home into me, and make visual and visceral my holy purposefulness, to bathe the world in the golden music of Divine Love.

I am my dream come true. I am my hero. And my Higher Self has a plan. *Onward!*

~o~

37th Avenue Robin

The Universe knew that morning what I did not know, that I was stepping from a train and walking several blocks to meet with the dream and the destiny of all my lifetimes, to merge paths with the most important person I would ever know.

So the Universe asked the weather and one lovely being to help me.

At the last block, the sidewalk suddenly ended in a strange grouping of some dozen holes in the ground, big enough to sink my foot into. And the early morning rain had made puddles of all the holes.

I have quite limited eyesight but I could see there were pothole pitfalls. I turned to walk in the street instead, and saw ten or more cars driving slowly toward me. Back to the holey sidewalk.

I stood looking at the holes, wondering how to navigate them.

"C'mon," a Robin said in a Robin voice. "It's all right."

I couldn't see where the Robin was but I could hear that he was quite near. "C'mon" he said again.

"Will you please tell me if I'm about to walk into a hole?" I asked the Robin out loud.

"It's all right," Robin answered.

"Please help me." I moved one foot toward what might be a safe spot, and stopped, waiting for Robin to speak.

"C'mon."

I stepped, on solid ground. Next foot.   I paused.

"It's all right" he said.

I stepped. Safe. Next try. "C'mon." Safe. Next. "It's all right." Safe.

I waited before each step, and Robin advised me. Surely the most amazing walk of my life!

After safely passing the last pthole, I started to say "Thank you" when Robin flew up saying, I think, "Well, that was fun!" and flew down the street. I felt such gratitude and delight, knowing completely that the Universe had sent that Robin to help me.

The meeting with the most important person I would ever know was momentous. In fact, it was the start of all my dreams coming true.

After the meeting I walked out smiling and feeling deeply happy, and lighter.

At the front of the building a little sparrow was rummaging in a flowering bush and singing a sparrow song. I laughed and thanked the little bird for his melody.

Walking back onto the street of the potholes, for some reason I felt an urge to look up. Sitting on a wire, there he was. Robin. When I looked up at him, he began laughing. He laughed and laughed, chuckling and giggling like a child.

My Robin. Making me laugh too. Making certain I was paying absolute attention to this day, to the joy, to the presence of the Universe at my side. Making certain I would remember always that on this day I stepped safely and surely into my destiny, into eternity.

~O~

The Mirror Me - 2

"I love you, me." I practice an exercise my Spiritual Teacher taught me, to strengthen self-acceptance and self-love.

My eyes look back to me from the mirror, holding my gaze as though listening intently.

"Who comes to me now?" they ask. "The yearning child? The worried grownup? The one who believes in herself? The one who wonders if she can?"

"I come to you," I replied, "as the me who wants to know, at last, how to find the truth about me. I want to know how to identify truth-me, see truth-me, know truth-me. I want to live as truth-me, with no more masks, no more pretenses, no more walls. That pretend-me is exhausting to maintain. No more. I want to find and be the me I truly am."

"That, my love, my self, is the easiest question you have ever asked me," said my eyes.

"Tell me!"

"My love, my self, you find the truth about you by paying attention to how you feel emotionally. Every moment. Every day. Always."

"Paying attention to my feelings? What do you mean?"

"Finding your truth is simple. When you feel content, joyful, merry, enthusiastic, appreciating, grateful, goofy, laughing, alive -- you are living your truth. *That* is the true you."

"So many emotions..."

"My love, my self, they are just different ways to spell 'love', love of you for you."

"Do you mean when my insides feel relaxed and happy? When I smile or laugh for almost no reason?"

"Yes, my love, my self. When you choose what you love instead of what you do not love. When you choose what makes your heart sing. And when you stay in a state of joy, *that* is your truth-you."

"I get it! I get it. Thank you. But sometimes I don't feel those wonderful feelings. Sometimes I feel angry, or resentful, impatient or worried, or sad, or even afraid or despairing. All the negative feelings, I've known them well."

"Do you enjoy those feelings?"

"No! But I'm used to them. I've known them for so long. Is that wrong?"

"There is no 'wrong' feeling. There is only *is*. If you don't enjoy what you're feeling, can you think of a way out?"

"Uh, thinking about something else? Replacing the thought that I don't like with thoughts that I do like? A Spiritual Teacher taught me that feelings are caused by thoughts, and how we feel is because of what we're thinking about."

"Yes! Pay attention. Choose! If feeling bad doesn't feel good, stop the train of thought you're on, and transfer to a thought about something you love, enjoy, delight in, treasure, admire. If I had fingers I would snap them now because it's just that fast. Snap! You can change the way you feel by deliberately changing what you're thinking about. Snap!"

"That sounds wonderful. But sometimes my mind just rolls on and on."

"Pay attention. Pay attention to you. My love, my self, this is your life and it's yours to shape and color and sing. To do that, pay attention to how you feel and what you are thinking about. Notice. Observe. Choose."

"Why do you keep calling me 'my love, my self'? Who are you?"

"You."

"Do you mean I am my love, my self?"

"Yes, my love, my self."

"You are my Higher Self, aren't you, this voice not spoken but known?"

"Yes. I have other really cool names. Divine Love. Universal Consciousness. You. Me."

"Me. My love, my self..."

~o~

Serendipity

Serendipity was my Buddha cat. I had not known there could be such a thing, but for seventeen years I knew he had come to teach me how to be the human I aspired to be.

Dipity was a funny Master Teacher. Round, not overweight just ungraceful, kind of galumphing. He was merry, goofy, suddenly insanely playful, adventurous, always sweet, devoted and affectionate.

Fearless he was, the first of the four cats in the family to try something new and potentially risky. He was the first to try jumping to the top of the shower sliding door frame and walking back and forth along that narrow structure. He would push his tail against the ceiling for leverage. The other cats always watched him to see how to do something new.

With surprising depth, he would curl up beside

me and listen to Wagnerian operas with me. Who knew?

Dipity kept me in an uninterrupted state of being loved. My favorite moment of the day was in the morning just before I came fully awake from dreams. Every morning without fail, as my awareness was beginning to gather, I would hear the start of a purr, like a motor starting up, near my face.

As I opened my eyes, I was looking into two very pale blue eyes in a grey-taupe face very close to mine. His face radiated happiness and love, and that's how I started every day. Magnificent.

I described him as "love walking", and he taught me how to *be* patience, forgiveness, absolute devotion, and goofy abandon. By being who he was, he showed me, day by day in real life, how to be loving and fearless.

One week I noticed he was losing weight. His doctor's tests confirmed his slow kidney failure. After a brief hospital stay, he came home and I knew, and I'm certain he knew too, our life together was coming to an end.

He and his best bud-cat Clearlight Dancing played and napped together, and he and I played and napped together. Love filled the air in our home.

One Friday in Spring as I sat at my desk, I watched a slim Serendipity jump up on to the loveseat in front of Dancing and do something he had never done before. He licked the bridge of Dancing's nose the way a mother cat does, three times. And I knew he was saying a final "I love you" to Dancing. I was so moved that he let me watch this intimate event. Dancing immediately licked Dipity back like a mother cat, saying a final "I love you".

Then Dipity, the love of my life, turned his head and looked in my eyes, some six feet away from me.

I heard a clear masculine voice say out loud, "It's time for me to go now".

"Okay, love," I answered in my mind.

I picked up the phone and called his doctor and caught the office just before it closed for the evening. We made an appointment for the next morning.

Dipity moved on out of the physical that next morning, easily, quickly, in my arms.

When I left the animal hospital I donated his carrying case to them and I knew he would have approved.

Instead of driving, I had taken a taxi to the doctor's office knowing I wouldn't be sane enough to drive home. So I walked, empty-handed, to the bus stop to go home.

Waiting for a bus, I felt my life had ended. How to live without that sweet, funny being who had lived for me?

Something moved. I turned and saw a movement again. A lady hummingbird had flown to a cherry blossom tree in full bloom, only a couple of feet from me.

A hummingbird! I hadn't seen or thought of hummingbirds in forty years! In Spirit Animal lore and dream symbolism, Hummingbird Spirit represents joy and it is a bringer of joy.

I instantly, deeply, knew that Dipity had sent that

hummingbird to me! Not twenty minutes after he left the physical, Dipity sent me a gift of joy. Still my teacher, he was telling me to choose not sadness but joy.

In the years since he left his body, he has sent me hummingbirds in odd places at odd times, and I can feel his beautiful furry hand on my shoulder. I smile and, out loud, say "Thank you, love". And I see his pale, pale blue eyes smiling at me.

~o~

Imperfect, While Perfect

"I love you."

"I love you, too."

"I want to be perfect for you."

"You *are* perfect for me, my love."

"No, no, I'm not perfect. I know my intentions are kind and compassionate. But sometimes I could do things better. I'm not perfect."

"But, love, don't let yourself feel confused. The Earthly manifestation of you that I'm leaning against right now *cannot* be perfect. That's a basic rule of this game, that in physical manifestation, in a life on Earth, in the Third Dimension, we are, *by definition,* imperfect."

"That's what I'm saying!"

"Okay. But the beings we *truly* are, the spiritual beings we are, who are our eternal selves, are perfect. You know that there is nothing in Creation that is not perfection, because everything emanates from Ultimate Perfection. You are perfection. I am perfection. In essence, everything is perfection."

"Well if I'm such a perfect being, why don't I remember to put the cap back on the toothpaste, and why do I leave the bag of groceries sitting in the kitchen and forget for hours to put them away?"

"Because, my love, the toothpaste-user and the groceries-putter are the Earthly manifestation. Imperfect. Impatient. Imprecise. Impetuous. Imprudent. Improvident. Implacable. Oh this is fun! Imperious."

"Improvable! Ha! Yes, improving from imperfect to impeccable."

"Oh that's so good! Love, our Earth job here is to live integrated, balanced spiritual-and-physical lives, and smile at the slip-ups and pat ourselves on the back when we flow smoothly."

"Why do you put up with my slip-ups?"

"Because you shine. And I am shinier because I'm around you. You radiate light and love. You are, you know, the current manifestation of the glorious being who is eternally perfect, and eternally adorable, and eternally fun to be with. And I love all of you together, right here, right now."

"You're the best. C'mon, let's go to sleep."

"And you're the best, too. Let's remember to put toothpaste on the shopping list, okay? Goodnight, sweetheart."

"G'night, sweetheart."

~o~

Halos Of Sound

In a wonderful mentored group for the development of intuitive abilities, the Spiritual Teacher always began the exercises with a marvelous, deep, guided meditation.

The Mentor began by softly playing an F-note, or Heart Chakra note, Crystal Singing Bowl. The sound of Crystal Singing Bowls is pure, clear, clean, focused, and always delights me in a rising, uplifting way.

One day I was, as usual, contentedly starting the meditation. My eyes were closed, my being aware and relaxed.

As the sound of the Singing Bowl lightly rose and fell, rose and fell, swam in and out of near-silence, the communication between the Bowl and me changed.

Behind my closed eyes, clairvoyantly I saw rings

of colors begin to radiate slowly from the Bowl. First a ring of clear sky blue, then rose, then golden-white.

The rings floated gently from the Bowl, like ripples of water on a smooth lake, undulating, shimmering blue and rose and golden-white in the spiritual air all around the Bowl.

She was sharing her life with me, this lovely Bowl, smiling and showing me the auras of her Song, breathing beauty to me, entering with me an ethereal dance of light and sound.

~O~

The Raphael Frequency

Angels and Archangels were never part of my awareness until one year when I realized that the Angels Themselves had begun teaching me who They are, while helping me learn who I am.

Since everything that exists is energy, everything is a unique vibrational frequency, just like me. We call one frequency Archangel Raphael who helps us heal problems that are physical, mental, emotional or spiritual, the whole spectrum of our existence.

I had a thing happen to my right lung and the right chamber of my heart. Actually, what happened was that I experienced an emotional heartbreak. We store grief in our lungs, and my physical heart and my lung began the process of expressing my emotional heart.

I did the ER, OR, ICU and recuperative nursing home adventure for a month. I had asked if a Reiki practitioner was available, but none was. So alone in my room every day I requested, out loud, the support and healing of the Archangels Who felt like friends to me.

I asked Archangel Raphael, the Healer, to bring to me divine healing energy and help my body heal itself.

All the doctors were amazed at how quickly and easily I healed. But it didn't seem like such a big deal to me because I knew I had great resources within my intentions and my relaxed feelings about my body, as well as spectacular "outside" help, spiritual help, which the doctors could not see.

So when the cardiologist ordered an echo-cardiogram I felt no more than the tiniest wisp of concern, not even worry and certainly not fear.

The electrodes around my torso tickled a bit. Before starting the test, the lab person stepped out for a few minutes, leaving me alone in the test room.

I started to ask for Archangel Raphael's support. I saw in front of me and a couple of feet above me in the room, a thick, shimmering deep green flow, like a slowly-moving draping garment, and I felt throughout my being a sudden gentle stream of love and peacefulness and confidence.

Archangel Raphael. He was in the room, protecting me, comforting me, and helping me.

In his flowing deep green manifestation, he stayed through the echo-cardiogram and I felt completely safe. The test, by the way, showed that my heart had "somehow" reversed its condition and was now totally normal. Healed.

As I walked out of the test room, I could feel a presence of great strength and loving companionship beside me. And I saw this presence moving with me, a shimmering, flowing frequency in deep green.

A deep green frequency in the cosmic music, as I am my deep turquoise frequency in the cosmic music. And together we walked out into the January day, the sun shining, our frequencies harmonizing.

~o~

Changing The Future

This is easier than I expected it would be, isn't it? It turns out to be all about choosing.

I changed my past by the energy of my desire, my intention, my thoughts and feelings. I can change my future the same way!

All that I want for me is here, right now, *within me*, in what I am being right now. If I am kind and loving and merry, I am radiating kindness and love and laughter from me into the world and into the Universe.

So I am creating a path using my desire and my intention. I am paving that path with my feelings and beliefs, my thoughts, what I say and what I do.

I am making my future right now, from within me, from how I am right now. And if I would prefer to be different from who I am right now, I change me right now, and the instant I do that I create a new path with new paving!

What I am is what I become. If I love what I am, I'm creating a future me that I will love. If I do not love aspects of what I am, I can change those aspects by replacing them with the ways I prefer to be, that make me feel good about being me. And I will become what I have thus created.

It's all in my hands, isn't it? I am the constantly-unfolding creator of me. And therefore the constantly-unfolding me is created by me.

What I send out, comes back to me, because the Law of Attraction says that what is like unto itself is drawn. What I send out attracts that which is exactly like it to come back to me. Sso more of that comes to me.

My kindness and understanding bring me kindness and understanding from others. My anger brings me anger from others. My sadness brings me sadness. My hugging brings me hugging. My encouragement of others brings me encouragement from others.

I send out honesty, I receive honesty. I send out criticism, I receive criticism. I send out the willingness to be patient, I receive patience.

What is like unto itself is drawn. What I send out attracts that which is exactly like it to come back to me.

I choose. What I am radiates from me in all directions, bathing Earth in what I am, bathing humanity in what I am. And the me who will be a minute from now or an hour from now or a day from now, I am radiating from me right now, into my future. I am creating me, as I go along.

As I choose to change, I change who I will be. I change future me. I change my future. I change everything, because everything is energy, driven by desire, intention, thoughts, beliefs, feelings, words and actions. And I control all of that inside me!

So I am my own creation! And with every thought, intention, feeling, action, I am creating my future!

~o~

Sugar Maple Tree

Out of the blue one day, the Sugar Maple Tree Spirit who is one of my Guardian Spirits told me what follows in a happy burst of expression.

Deep in Winter, the Sugar Maple Tree is curled quietly into herself like a sleeping cat. She is in a long, serene semi-meditative stillness.

In early Spring she stirs, stretches her arms in all directions, looks around, and notices the changes in her world since she went to quiet.

There's a new house being built. A baby came forth. An old man who patted her when he walked past moved on out of the physical. And neighbors who didn't speak are now happy to plan a barbecue together.

Sugar Maple Tree opens her heart and her skin to receive Father Sun. Every day, all day, she takes in his warmth and goodness and sweetness, and his gift of life.

During Summer, she becomes stronger, taller, even happier and wiser, learning new ways in the world as Sun shares with her his strength and his love. She welcomes his strength and his love, making him part of who she is.

In Autumn, Sugar Maple Tree celebrates her divine external expansion of consciousness and of their union. She rejoices by radiating new beauty, first in the color of the Sun. Then she sings in her own colors, melodies and harmonies and the richness of full orchestration.

She calls out, and shouts, and sings her joy in being Sugar Maple Tree, in being eternally beautiful, in being loved by Sun, in being a divine instrument to give delight and sweetness to the Earth and all who live here.

And then, her union with Sun begins a rest.

During Winter, Sugar Maple Tree holds herself contented and still, curled quietly into herself like a sleeping cat, thinking, feeling, planning, knowing all is well throughout the Universe forever.

~O~

Guardian Spirit

Shamanic journeys, I had read, can change one's life for the beautiful, for the wise. A shamanic journey is a wondrous exploration of Consciousness, including the consciousness of Earth and the beings who choose to inhabit earthly forms for a while.

I had experienced one such journey, a short one, with lovely results which told me important information about myself and helped me to understand myself better.

So when I learned that a Shamanic Practitioner who was greatly admired would be guiding a certain journey in my area, I leapt at the chance to participate. I am Tree-ness, with four planets in Taurus in my natal chart! The shamanic journey was intentioned to meet one's Medicine Tree. I couldn't wait!

In the journey, I met my Tree, a tall, lush, vigorous and beautiful Sugar Maple Tree. She and I experienced a long period of sweet, loving communication during the journey. In this flow of consciousness between us, my body merged into her body, into her bark and trunk and branches and leaves.

Tree and I felt deep safety and love and timelessness together. When the Shamanic Practitioner guided the participants to end and release our experiences, Tree and I separated, and looked at each other in smiles and heppiness.

After the journey, the shamanic guide told me that the merging I had experienced was proof that my Medicine Tree had become, in that moment, a Guardian Spirit for me, one of my protectors. Tree would guard me from unpleasant or dangerous people and intrusions.

I was thrilled! I could see clearly, still, this beautiful New England Sugar Maple who had come to me of her own free will, to stay with me and protect me. Such beauty! She was tall and powerful, lush with branches and twigs and leaves spreading wide and high. With me she is, I thought. I live in a reality of sweetness and strength.

Some weeks later, a friend and I got on a bus to go to a workshop. We sat in the very front seats on the bus, the better to see everything.

As my friend and I chatted, the bus stopped and a man got on who muttered curses and slammed his money into the fare machine. He sat opposite us, only a few feet away, and shouted his anger at the world.

His undirected fury got louder and his energy felt chaotic, ragged, sharp-edged, red. On he cursed, and I felt my friend becoming tense.

Out of the blue, I suddenly thought of Medicine Tree, and in my mind I called on her to protect me and my friend.

Instantly she appeared in her etheric body, placing herself right in front of me, between me and the unruly man, filling the whole area where we sat.

Clairvoyantly I watched as she spread her branches to their fullest extension, then brought them together, and began aiming them toward the man who was still cursing and shouting to the air.

Push! Shove! Sweep! The man was being Tree-handled!

The man jumped up from his seat in anger, yelling that he wanted to get off the bus. My Medicine Tree push-push-pushed him to the door!

The bus stopped, the door opened, and out the man jumped, shouting and taking his rage with him.

I couldn't stop myself from laughing! I grinned and sent my gratitude and love to Sugar Medicine Tree.

She gathered her branches around her, shook the negativity from her leaves, and sat down quietly. My beautiful and fierce protector!

~o~

Promises To Keep

Little one, here is our other gift to you.

We have given life to your body, the garment you will wear for this adventure you are beginning on Earth. Now we will give your life our wisdom, and we will show you and teach you everything we know.

Big-city life, and rural farm life
The stars
Wild birds
Car engines
Making music, loving music
Sawing wood
Sewing
Politeness
Annual planting and harvesting of vegetables, fruits

and flowers
Independence and self-reliance
Cooperation and teamwork
Criticizing, judging
Solving puzzles and mysteries, reading maps and creating patchwork quilts
Equality
Hierarchy
Sharing
Keeping secrets, not sharing
Respect for animals, growing things, the land
Stubbornness
Patience
History
Geography
Love for your language
Arrogance
Math
Mechanics
Deep, unacknowledged anger
Criticism, humiliation and intimidation
Somewhat frequent beatings with a hardwood paddle

Very frequent hard face-slappings
Being organized, and planning successfully
Enjoying machines and tools, taking care of them
Helping less fortunate people
Helping to save endangered species
Emotional coldness and distance
Service to others
Unforgiveness
Doing what you love
An adventurous spirit
Conformity
Bigotry, exclusion
Responsibleness, dependability and stability
Fear of authority
Love of learning
Doing things with excellence
Fidelity
Humility
Simplicity
Quiet
Our religion
Our politics
Our definitions, assumptions, beliefs and

expectations
The deep closeness of the two of us.

    We two and you, together, agreed on this before
we all came into this incarnation, for our spiritual
development and for yours, beloved child of ours.
This is the costume, the personality, that the two of
us wear together this time.
    We offer you everything we are, everything you
will need to start your journey. This is the soul
contract we agreed upon with you, the roles we will
play this time, the playground and classroom we give
you. This we do in divine love for ourselves and for
you.
    You contracted that you will observe, absorb,
allow, resist, and learn.
    And you contracted to choose which of our gifts
fit you, that you will cherish, and which do not fit
you, that you will replace. For you are not us, nor
an extension of us. You are unique, and as you live
you will create a wisdom that looks just like you,
only you.

Godspeed, sweet child. We will do this thing together, the three of us, in Divine Love. And when we have all fulfilled our contracts, we'll be waiting for you with open arms. We'll see you on the other side of promises.

~o~

Story Stone

From a table scattered with interesting crystals and stones, polished and unpolished, I closed my eyes and reached to take a stone to scry, to read whatever spiritual message it might wish to tell me.

I touched a clear quartz polished stone, smaller than the palm of my hand and round. I picked it up, closed it in my hand, walked back to my chair and sat down.

As I opened my hand, the stone began to laugh to me!

It laughed so happily that I began laughing too. I looked at the smooth stone, and a Being appeared in the stone. Short like a young child, but not a child. He felt like masculine energy. He had a round head and a roundish body, and the surface of his body was a light brown color. I knew that the surface of his body was sort of fuzzy, a little like the surface of velvet.

I knew this was a Being from another planet.

Instantly I was out in space! Roaming, wandering, investigating out in space, enjoying the experience.

I was past the sky. Did the Being come to me from past the sky?

Stars and dust trails, waves and currents. What a calm and simple roaming. Serene and sweet. I was buoyant and floating, streaming in space.

My mind knew the words "Look up! Look up! Scry the sky! The cosmos is out there!"

In delight, in play and peacefulness, I looked to my hand and saw the plain, clear, round polished stone of quartz. And I saw the Being also.

I looked up and saw the room I was sitting in, and behind the room, around about the room, above the room, I saw the dark and starry space the Being had come from, where I had just wandered.

I knew the stone's intention was for me to keep looking differently, looking at me and at life differently, and to be sure to laugh. I found myself laughing which was raising my frequency, helping me to go up, which would help me to scry the sky.

~o~

To Fly

I want to fly!

In sleepdreams I fly. In daydreams I fly. In imaginings, I fly. In happiness, I fly. In love, I fly. In wonderings, I fly. In rolling laughter, I fly.

I have not yet flown in the air. I want to climb to the top of the tallest tree in the neighborhood, or the highest building in the neighborhood, and leap into the air and fly.

I've heard it said that I cannot fly in the air because the collective human consciousness does not believe that a human body can fly in the air. They say that theoretically, if enough people were to believe it can be done, they will radiate that belief into the world and into the Universe, and then it could be done.

Others say that I cannot do this because I myself do not believe a human body can fly in the air. So, theoretically, when I believe it I will be able to do it.

But I do believe! I can see it in my mind. I can see me flying in the air. I believe in magic. In divine magic. In thought magic. In emotion magic. In the magic of my own magicalness as a magical being. And I believe in flying.

I feel that believing is extremely important, a really powerful step in making happen what I want to happen. But I feel that the most important step is *knowing*. Not just believing I can fly, but knowing that magical me in my divine and beautiful and magnificent magicalness can fly in the air.

So, to start flying, how do I get from believing to knowing?

~0~

Firelight

As I did in many incarnations thousands and even hundreds of years ago, I sit cross-legged on the ground, poking a stick into the fire I have built, because it's fun to make the fire splash showers of sparks into the night.

My fire is well made, strong and bright. It keeps me warm as it radiates light in all directions, even into the Earth and into the Cosmos.

Deep within, this fire I have created feels brilliant and powerful. It has clarity and confidence. Self-worth. Self-love. Self-belief. Self-trust. Intentioned joy and laughter. The delight of being. The divine purposefulness of being itself.

My fire laughs and leaps, flashing red and oranges and yellows and bits of white. The colors are music dancing with the deep, quiet indigo of the endless Cosmos which surrounds me. My fire hums a steady Song of security and adventure.

Even so, I know what is out there.

Doubt is lurking out there, just beyond the reach of the firelight. Out where I cannot yet see it, doubt paces slowly and waits patiently, and sometimes sits unmoving and waits patiently.

Doubt is always watching me, ready to lunge toward me when I waiver from love of self, from trust in self, from trust in the Universe. When I waiver from the sweet sure powerfulness of knowing that I know what I know.

If I listen absolutely, I can just hear the quiet breath of doubt, out there. If I yield to the lurking danger, my fire will dim. Its warmth will flow away. I will become afraid.

If I surrender to the familiar seduction of doubt, I will become blinded to my fire.

But not for long.
 I can choose something better.
 I can raise my head to the indigo frequency

bathing me, and ask for help. Help will come, always and ever.

The Universe will offer to me, because I asked, a thin line of light. The Universe will offer to me the comfort and encouragement I offer to others.

And when I look in the direction of that light, I will remember that I know what I know. And the line of light will grow quickly, chasing after doubt. Light will be white, then yellows and oranges and red.

I will begin to see more clearly, and I will be able to choose to replace the doubting thought with the certain thought, the crushing thought with the rising thought. Because I do know that I know what I know, without doubt. And I do know that I light my way.

I am my fire. I am my brilliant and powerful light. And I am never alone. I am loved. All is well. The Universe is my friend, and the Universe has my back, always and ever. Together we get it right!

~O~

The Apu Speaks

I had been in Peru for only a week at the start of a long sacred journey that I had created for myself. I knew in my bones that I was one of the returning Children Of The Light. As for what that knowing would actually mean, what the sacredness would turn out to be, I was not sure. But I knew the Universe would show me, because all the planning had unfolded as smoothly as a blossoming flower.

Settling into my window seat on a one-hour flight from Juliaca, Peru going north to Cuzco, I noticed that the cabin of the plane seemed to be full yet quiet, with people who spoke together very softly or mused alone.

From my window I watched the shining white clouds not far below us hiding the Andes Mountains, then decided to stop blinding myself from the sun-bright whiteness of the clouds.

I settled back and began reading a book. I loved the book and in the quiet I quickly slipped into the story.

Suddenly, out of the blue, my body was shaken very quickly three times, back, forth, back, as though someone were shaking me by my shoulders, quickly but carefully.

Trouble? A fast glance around me. No one was stirring. No surprise, no anxiety. No sound, just the steady hum of the engines. Nothing.

Then he spoke emphatically. *"Pay attention to me!"* A clear masculine voice, insistent, even commanding.

Instantly I knew.

I looked out the window. There he was, Mount Ausungaté, the sacred mountain of the Andes, his Spirit, his Apu, speaking to me.

He was so close across the clouds, taller than the clouds, as white as the clouds. He stood, his head and shoulders above the clouds, looking at me. Robust, deeply powerful, ancient, looking at me.

My eyes filled with tears of joy. He had shaken me. Or the Universe had shaken me. Same thing.

He had spoken to me. Or the Universe had spoken to me. Same thing.

What a gift I had just been given!

The Apu, the Spirit, manifesting in that high, majestic mountain, was instructing me to be present and mindful, the foundation of being able to be loving and compassionate with myself and all life.

I knew I would hear his voice clearly as I roamed Peru.

As the plane kept moving north, past him, I turned away from the window smiling, the sight of Mt. Ausungaté just over there, forever in my eyes, the Apu's voice forever in my mind. I am so blessed! The sacred mountain spoke to me!

~O~

How To Trust,
In One Easy Lesson

Blue blue sky everywhere. Hot air. Hot. Hot.
The sand under my bare feet is hot and crunchy,
and my feet sink slightly into the sand as I run
toward little waves at the edge of vast blue. I can't
see the end of this blue which meets a horizon of
blue. The world is all blue. Where meets where,
and where do they meet?

Ahhhh. Cool water hits my toes, my feet, my
ankles. Oh yum! Cool ocean covers the skin of my
legs, my belly, and I sink into her in surrender to this
blissful softness.

I swim, a bit aimlessly, grateful to the ocean for
accepting me, grateful she allows me to become part
of her, grateful for this embrace of different species.
Ahh this feels so good!

The ocean is peaceful today. I decide to float.

Will I remember how to float? It's been so many years. Do I remember?

I twirl front over back over front over back, folding out of the water, then being part of the water. I feel tall and very elegant like a loose stalk of wild, willowy seaweed. Will a Sea Otter, who probably calls herself Amethyst, come and wrap herself in me on the skin of the ocean and go to sleep?

A bit of salt water gets in my mouth and I spit it out. Pulling up my legs from inside the ocean I flatten out my body from toetip to headtip. I am a motionless strand of kelp.

I float!

Is the ocean floating me? Or is my belief in floating floating me? Or are the ocean and I, inseparably together, are we floating me?

Like tiny leaps of faith, little rhythmic rolls of ocean rise me and fall me on their way to the shore. Rise me. Fall me. So small, the laps against my body are almost silent.

I am embraced. The world's largest ocean is holding me gently in her strong and flowing hands.

Or is my body holding her around me?

I open my eyes, and see only blueness. I am nowhere. Ever so slightly I am rising and falling in nowhere, bluewhere, leaps of faithwhere. I am goal-less, riding effortlessly in the flow. Attachments released. Memories floating away like balloons into the sky. Detatched. Beingness.

I float, and I feel happy, quietly happy. I accept. I allow. I float. I give myself to my happiness. I float. I surrender into my happiness. Being happiness, being now, I am in peace. I am safe in my happiness. All is well. I love who I am being. I believe.

Giving myself to my happiness, being my happiness, I become trust.

Am I trusting the ocean? Am I trusting me? Am I trusting the Universe? Is there any difference?

~O~

Apparition

Up at 5:00 AM. Still dark. Looking out the window of my *casita* I saw only dark, dense jungle greenery of the Peruvian cloud forest.

This was a very, very special day, when I would meet with my Q'ero Shaman, descendant of the ancient Inca high priests. I would go to Machu Picchu with him and create a *despacho*, an offering of gratitude to Spirit.

I felt humble that I had been especially chosen to be with Don Nazario Turpo, chief Shaman of the Inca shamanic lineage. He was the shamanic steward of Ausungaté, the great mountain of the Andes, and of the Apu, or Spirit, of that mountain.

A guide met me at my hotel lobby. I

spoke English and almost no Spanish. My guide spoke English and Spanish. Don Nazario's guide spoke Spanish and Quechwa, the Native Andean language. Don Nazario spoke Quechwa. Fun!

Our walk to meet with Don Nazario was on a road covered entirely in cobblestones that had been worn smooth for more than five hundred years . An early shopkeeper walked past us and the only vehicle was a bicycle.

A few dim streetlamps and the late full moon lit our way. My guide and I talked about 15th-Century Pachakutiq's visionary spiritual leadership of the Inca Empire, and about the current start of the cleansing of Mother Earth and the opening of portals to other Dimensions during the Fifth World.

Suddenly out of the blue a semi-white cat ran slowly, diagonally, in front of us almost on top of our feet, cutting us off. I grabbed my guide's arm to stop him and we stood completely still.

This cat was round, short-haired but fluffy, and his fur wasn't white like fur but white like light. He was luminous!

A few feet from us, the cat quickly scampered just like a squirrel up a short wood post. He stopped, clinging there, and looking back at me, and he smiled.

Dipity!

My Serendipity, my Buddha cat who taught me how to be a good human, the love of my life, who had moved on out of the physical exactly two years before.

When he was in the physical and wore a body, it was round and his fur was short but extremely fine and fluffy. I used to kid him about his body, telling him, "You're not fat, you're fluffy!"

In our home he loved dashing in front of my toes and cutting me off. When he scampered up wood posts at home I always laughed and told him he was a squirrel. And when he got to the top he always clung there on four sets of claws, looked back at me, and smiled. Dipity!

The luminous cat on this cobblestone road jumped from the wood post to the top of a short wall beside the post, just a few feet off the ground, and looked at me, radiating merry delight and love.

He closed his eyes as cats do when they are sending a kiss. I sent him my love, and felt his love for me wave toward me and around me.

"That was an apparition. Let's go," said my Andean guide as he began to walk. I glanced back. The luminous cat was looking toward me, smiling, eyes half-closed in contentment. I wrapped him in the energy of my love as I walked away.

Dipity had been sending hummingbirds to me since a few minutes after he left the physical. An hour after the apparition on the cobblestone road, the Shaman and I were conducting the *despacho* ceremony at the edge of Machu Picchu.

A hummingbird, whose Medicine is joy, who never sits still, sat quietly for almost a half-hour in a very young tree only an inch behind me, blessing me and the ceremony.

~O~

I'm In Good Hands

The flu? I didn't know what I had, but I knew I was quite sick. So one mid-November day, off I went to see the doctor.

In her reception area I waited while the receptionist completed a phone call.

Suddenly, the first six notes of a song I loved when I heard it living abroad and have never heard in the U.S. were in the air. A wondrous, sparkling, beautiful song, whose lyrics I knew well. They told of friends gliding through the air together, safe and happy.

Someone's cell phone was the instrument that the Universe was using to speak to me through the song.

"That music!" I called out. A woman held her phone up and raised the volume. "I haven't heard that song," I said, "since I lived in Japan years ago. I love that song!"

I had sung the song dozens of times years ago. The lyrics of love and fun and comfort flowed through my mind, and I began to sing softly, smiling.

I loved hearing and singing the song again! I loved being inside the song.

Then everything changed.

Over the reception desk and the furniture and the windows in the office, I saw in a fluid stream many, many Beings of Light, who I knew were my Angels and Spirit Guides, all in white, riding the air.

They were loving me, smiling to me, floating in front of me, around me, all looking at me, touching my hair, touching my arms, holding my hands, smiling smiling smiling to me, wrapping me in love and light. Floating. Flying. Loving me.

I noticed the desk and the windows again. The song was coming to the end.

I knew throughout my being, I knew absolutely, I knew that I am safe, I am well taken care of, and I am in good hands.

For the first time in my life, I truly felt that I belonged in my life, that I belonged being me, and that all is well throughout the Universe.

I was right. Events in my life during the next weeks, and months, and two years, were mostly surprises, sometimes not what I wanted. Relationship surprises. Medical surprises. Spiritual self-questioning surprises.

During those two years I felt great sorrow, and I cried, and I yelled to the Universe. But I kept remembering the power and the beauty, the sweetness and all the love, of the message to me, and so I wasn't afraid or despairing.

And I came through that time loving me fully at last, loving my life fully at last, and knowing fully that I am safe, I am well taken care of, and I am in good hands.

I knew this because the Universe told me so, I paid attention, I believed It, and together I and the Universe made it so.

~O~

Believe In The Little White Boat

Having brought to this incarnation lots of cardinal signs and other astrological leadership strengths, I always used to want everything NOW. Now now now, no waiting, no standing in line, no "Be a good girl and sit there quietly", no "Everything comes to those who --" ARRGHH!

Then one year after receiving several sessions of Reiki healing, I felt more open and relaxed and happy. I began to notice that the Universe was actually around me, walking hand in hand with me, showing me, in big events and little events, that I am safe and loved.

I began to accept that I'm not doing this life thing alone. That life is offered by the Universe, chosen by me and shaped by me, step by step, and that I have help all along the way.

I began to feel that there is a "timing" that is not mine, not human, not of Earth. That the events of my life were slipping into place without my management, and were surprises that were usually lovely and always interesting.

Beauty showed up without my planning it.

Sweetness spread to me without my having done anything to beckon it.

Love walked up to me and put its arms around me, even though I had not expected it.

Challenges and obstacles began to show themselves clearly as not horrible things but opportunities to choose what I really want to believe and be.

Healing, of my lifelong sadness, fears, and negative reactions, showed up, in the forms of deeply helpful people, laughter and insights, and asked, "How may I serve you?"

Wisdom and truth kept tapping me on the shoulder, pointing to what I should pay attention to.

That sounds a bit mystical, and that's exactly what I experienced. Surprises and gifts came from the Universe.

And the more I opened my hands to receive, and my mind to understand, and my heart to trust, the more gifts showed up. The more I smiled and felt "I'll try this", the more fun I had living.

I saw there is a Divine Timing managed by the Universe, Source, God, Creator, Isness, Beingness, Cosmic Consciousness, It, They.

Since They live in the vast indigo-blueness, They see all, which I cannot see from where I am. They see the big picture of my life and my soul, which I cannot see. They see what must come before what in my life, which I cannot see. They know all the whys and the becauses, the whens, wheres and hows, which I cannot know.

So I must trust. That was very difficult for me at first, accepting that someone knew my highest good better than I did. I think that a deep and ancient fear inside me expected me to be killed or sent insane if I did not hold on tightly to every big and small aspect of my life.

But over a fairly short period of time, it became obvious that They really knew what They were doing and I was feeling not killed or insane but happier and happier about what life was presenting to me. I was feeling smarter, lighter, clearer and more powerful. And I was laughing more than I ever had in my life and I just plain felt good.

They are really good at offering beings, events and circumstances that make my heart sing. In the right timing, in Divine Timing.

It became easy, if I let it be easy.

I visualized myself stepping into a small, lovely white rowboat. No oars necessary because I don't have to control the boat. My sweet little white boat and I are drifting gently down a flowing stream, never far from either bank, always safe.

As I and my boat float, I can watch on the banks the seahorses dance and twirl together, and the young dragons play hopscotch among the rainbow-colored flowers.

I trail my fingers in the silvery water of the stream as we flow.

Just as I feel hungry, I see a little table jutting out into the stream and it holds a thick, yummy-looking sandwich. As I pass by I pick up the sandwich and see that it's made of my favorite sandwich things including a kosher dill pickle!

Just ahead is another little table holding napkins, a jar of gourmet mustard and a small butterknife, and I bring them into my boat.

Soon I see a glass of water. And then grapes and raspberries and sliced kiwis! Yippee!

Isn't it amazing, I marvel to myself, what happens when I stay in the flow? When I allow Them to provide for me? They offer me such terrific stuff! Everything comes to me in its right time.

This little white boat is my friend, and I will ride in it in patience and simplicity, and I will care for it lovingly. We flow on.

I am in charge, because this is my life, a life of free will. The Light Beings who know me so well offer, and I choose what I will accept.

I am in charge, so They take what I choose and weave, new thread by new thread, the fabric that I keep creating as my life.

Now and then I start to slip a bit, back into the old way of expecting that I must know everything and plan everything and do everything and control everything. That I am the only one who will look out for me. I've found that that way is exhausting, and actually boring. The Universe's surprises and gifts turn out to be much more fun and fulfilling.

So I step back into my little white boat, and flow.

I trust. Now I know there is Divine Timing. I know I am in good hands. I know I am never alone. I can breathe, calmly and quietly.

And feel Them smile with me as something beautiful and loving beckons to me.

I and my little white boat flow on.

~o~

In The Field Beyond Forgiveness

I love you unconditionally. I love you without doubt or hesitation, without question or reservation. I love you because you are. I love you because I am. I love you because I love you.

And so I forgive you, for everything, for all time, forever, because I choose to love and stay in this divine vibrational frequency of joyous, innocent union with me and with you, watching us both blossom and fly.

This condition of loving bliss was not easy for me as a human to achieve, but it is very knowable and very doable, with intention, choice and practice. The most important intention was to truly love myself, and then all else became possible. And the reward is sheer delight, a kind of grounded, practical, minute-by-minute floating fun!

Because I have been practicing this love, first for me then for you, one day I found that there is a place *beyond* forgiveness!

"Beyond right and wrong there is a field. I will meet you there," said the Sufi poet Rumi who knew that true human love is actually divine love expressing through each person.

There is a field beyond right and wrong, beyond forgiveness. There is the knowing that everything we do and say, think and feel, is all part of the path each of us choses to walk in this incarnation. By living our lives, we are doing the work we came here to do, learning who we are, and choosing who we desire to be -- and in that process, learning how to love ourselves.

And so, there is nothing that was wrong, and so nothing to forgive. We are doing our work. We are expressing Source, in the aspect of each individual with our talents and ancient soul histories, our beliefs and expectations.

Since we are thus, what is there to forgive? Since we are Source expressing as us and exploring as us, what is right or wrong?

I love me. I am. I love you. You are. Let us meet in the field of no comparison, no judgment, no analysis. Let us meet in the field of Isness and innocence. Let us Be together, in floating fun.

~o~

Sacred Phoenix

I dreamed that I saw you rising from the high, high summit of the holy mountain you had just climbed. I watched you rising, rising effortlessly in your completely open heart and your complete invincibility, rising from the top of your holy mountain, leaving a trail of sparkling silver light.

As you rose into the indigo, falling away from your perfect feet were old shackles of metal and leather. With your muscular hands and powerful intention and intense desire, you had broken open the shackles, releasing them from your perfect feet as you crumbled the rusted metal and rotted leather to dust, sending it into the indigo to become a different energy, to serve a new design.

I watched you rising like a wave, your bright and curious body radiating beams of green light, heart light, healing light, in all directions. Your ancient silken robe in wide stripes of vibrant blue and brilliant yellow rippled over your body as the air parted to give you passage. I saw the streams of green flowing from your body, from your robe.

I watched your violet wings immense and strong protecting you, giving you lift. I watched your beautiful hair float over your shoulders and down your back. I saw the ribbons of green wafting from your beautiful hair and violet wings, changing the indigo.

I watched you meander among clouds, your bright and clever hands now patting the top of a cloud while you and the cloud laughed together, now opening a cloud to twirl your body through, and the cloud and you, tickled, giggled.

I watched you rising into the indigo dotted everywhere with bits of gold and silver light. As you raised your hands to touch them, the stars smiled to you and waved to you, flew to wrap themselves around you, holding you in sweet and caressing love.

I watched you swell with joy that you arrived there. I watched you bow your head in gratitude that you arrived there.

I watched you look about, and heard you speak.

"There is only beauty to behold now, for all is of

my artistry.

"I want more. I am worthy of all. I want new and beautiful. Where do I go now for new and beautiful?"

I heard the Voice of the Indigo reply.

"The choice is ever yours, my hero, my love, my self. What shall we create?"

And the stars, smiling to your eyes, dancing with you as you held their hands in yours, the stars sang with you your name to all Creation.

~o~

Light Laughing

I am an Energy Medicine practitioner, also known as a Reiki Master healer. Frequently I conduct distance healing sessions. That means I'm in my home sending healing divine energy to a person or an animal who is at a distance, in their home, for example, or in a hospital, or off somewhere on vacation.

I really love doing distance healing. I tend to do this very late at night when the subject of the session is asleep and I communicate directly with their soul.

Just beautiful Universal Life Energy going on.

One night when I was doing this, I was sending healing energy to first one subject and then to another. And I was loving so much what I was doing that I didn't want to stop! I remembered a suggestion my Reiki Teacher had made, that once in a while we might want to send healing energy to our

Spirit Guides and Angels.

"Yes! That's what I'll do!" I decided.

I made the appropriate preparations and turned my intention and attention and action to, well, the air up in front of me.

The air instantly filled with scores or hundreds of Beings of Light, all white, all shining, crowding together, busy, some even carrying things like notebooks.

White! White! The air filled with white! Light shining shining shining!

All of Them were smiling or laughing, for me, to me. Light laughing. They made me laugh! And I kept sending Them Reiki energy, as I laughed and laughed with Them.

Well I'll be darned . So that's how the Universe, God, Source says thank you to us, by giving us a gift, laughter, that will help us raise our vibrational frequency and thus enhance our spiritual enlightenment. That is too cool! They thank us by giving to us what will benefit us the most.

Source rocks! And laughs.

~o~

Being The Song

What if everything is made of thoughts and desires and stardust? And what if everything could go with their best friend on an adventure past the planets, slip through the heliopause and out beyond our solar system into the rest of the Universe, on a journey that would last five billion years?

Sail on, Voyager 1 and Voyager 2 made of thoughts and desires and stardust. Sail on to seek and find and endlessly become. Say "Hi!" to Source for us.

We'll catch up with you when we've completed our learning and healing and becoming and having fun here.

We'll catch up with you when we remember that thought and desire created everything, and that our own thoughts and our own desires create everything.

~O~

I Am The Song

We are the Song, say the Voyager twins.

I am the Song, says the Crystal.

I am the Song, says Crabgrass.

I am the Song, says Crop Circle.

I am the Song, says Drought, says Hurricane.

I am the Song, says DNA.

I am the Song, says Electric Eel.

I am the Song, says Ethiopia.

I am the Song, says Sasquatch.

I am the Song, says ESP.

I am the Song, says Desk.

I am the Song, says Spaceship.

I am the Song, says Orion Nebula.

I am the Song, says 3.

I am the Song, says Particle.

I am the Song, says Wave.

I am the Song, says each. I am the Song, say all.

And the Song is Creation eternally Creator *ehyeh asher ehyeh* I am that I am Consciousness.

You are the Song.

A Game To Play:
Word Building, Source's Way

This is just a little game to practice seeing and being the way Creator sees and bes -- in love, encouragement and enthusiasm.

You put the *pow!* into empowerment.

You put the love into beloved.

You put the thy into empathy.

You put the us into trust.

You put the serve into observe.

You put the real into ethereal.

You put the <u>dance</u> into abundance.

You put the <u>light</u> into enlighten.

You put the <u>union</u> into communion.

You put the <u>infinite</u> into infinitesimal.

You put the <u>are</u> into awareness.

You put the <u>ability</u> into vulnerability.

You put the <u>in</u> into intimacy.

Your turn!

~O~

Ahhh uuu mmmmm

**the sound of the Universe,
the Song of everything**

Lora

How can someone whose eyesight is so limited
that she can hardly read, write a book? -- especially
one like this, rich in sensory experience. For years I
shook my fist at the sky because I cannot see clearly
forms and features, the physical. In time I found
that, instead, I am guided by the Universe to see
and know *the soul*, the essence, the truth of things,
by seeing them through my soul. Not *eye*-sight, but
in-sight. Not physical but *spiritual* reality,

consciousness -- which we can all see and know by changing what we expect to see... Not surface, but substance seen through our soul, which means seeing through the eyes of Source. *I Am The Song* proves that we can learn to see like that, and when we do life becomes magical and delicious.

"I want to know everything," I announced at age seven. Decades later, now I know that *choosing* is everything -- choosing how we see and understand reality, choosing intention, joy, forgiveness and love.

I've learned as singer, dancer, pianist, performer on stage, TV and radio, teacher, scholar, painter, mystic, author of short stories and poetry, advertising, travel and transcultural writer and editor, simultaneous interpreter, real estate agent, rural photographer, long-time resident of Japan and the U.S., short-time resident of Canada and Peru.

I am a Reiki Master healer, clairvoyant psychic, animal medium, spiritual counselor, cat whisperer and Earthbender. As an instrument of divine love and healing in the world, it is my honor and joy to share in clients' journeys of transcendence.

Made in the USA
Lexington, KY
25 October 2019

56051814R00199